SOULS EXIST
2ND EDITION

RICHARD SCHAIN

"There are only two questions for philosophy; the soul and God."

-- St. Augustine, *De Ordine*

Library of Congress Control Number : 2013910593

"Souls Exist," by Richard Schain ISBN 978-1-62137-314-8 (softcover), 978-1-62137-315-5 (ebook).

Published 2013 by Virtualbookworm.com Publishing Inc., P.O. Box 9949, College Station, TX 77842, US. ©2013, Richard Schain. All rights reserved. No part of this publication may be reproduced, stored in a retrieval system, or transmitted in any form or by any means, electronic, mechanical, recording or otherwise, without the prior written permission of Richard Schain.

Manufactured in the United States of America.

To Melanie
η μεγιστη ψυχη

Contents

Introduction i
1. The Soul Exists 1
2. The Human Condition 9
3. The Question of Reality 19
4. God, Soul and Søren Kierkegaard 24
5. The Impact of Culture 34
6. The Essence of Christianity 44
7. Creativity: Voice of the Soul 53
8. Personal Intuitions and Metaphysical Beliefs 64
9. The Materialist Ideology 76
10. Philosophy and Philosophers 83
11. The Materialist Worldview in America 93
12. A Cosmology for Souls 103
13. Intellectuals and Intellectuals Manqués 116
14. Philosophical Faith 129
Epilogue - 2nd Edition 139

Introduction

WE LIVE IN A society in which the material world and the real world are considered to be identical. As the title of this book indicates, it is about the reality of the soul, a subject that is not in high repute at this particular time in western intellectual history. I am neither 'priest nor professor' so it will become evident that the orientation is neither Christian nor scholarly; rather it represents the perspective of an independent thinker on a subject that was once near the top of the list of importance for the mentally developed person. One has only to glance through Etienne Gilson's *Spirit of Medieval Philosophy* to see how far contemporary society has fallen away from this concept. Consciousness of the soul is one of the casualties of the scientific worldview.

In addition to the topic of the soul (actually because of the nature of the subject), this writing has to do with creative expression and its relationship to the interior life of the individual. It is my conviction that a creative work *kata syneidēsin** does not require an audience—albeit one is not necessarily excluded—since its greatest benefit is the development of the soul of the creating person. More on this can be found in Chapter 7.

Epicurus, one of the most prolific of ancient philosophers (unhappily, virtually none of the writings of that remarkable man survived Christian obscurantism), was taken to task by the Stoic philosopher Epictetus for inconsistency in his attitudes. Epicurus' central doctrine was that pleasure was the ultimate virtue before which all other virtues must be accorded a lesser position. It is easy to see how the frankness of Epicurus caused him difficulty among the religiously minded Stoics and Christians, especially since his influence stubbornly persisted well into the Christian era. Epictetus, who was no Christian but might have easily been one with a few adjustments to his theology, discovered what he thought to be a glaring contradiction in the argument of Epicurus. How could Epicurus have labored so hard over so many books if his only concern was with pleasure?:

> Man, why do you take thought for our sake, why do you keep awake for us, why do you light your lamp, why do you rise early, why do you write such big books?

What the good Epictetus did not realize, since he was primarily a teacher not a writer, was that writing for Epicurus represented the ultimate pleasure, and the more he struggled and strained for the right phrases to express his thought, the more fulfilling writing was for him. Epicurus was one of the very few individuals in recorded history who began afresh in all the dimensions of mental activity. It must have been essential for him to objectify the whirl of thought and feelings of his fertile mind into coherent statements. Otherwise, his personality might have cracked into disjointed fragments as has been the case with many geniuses who could not impose order on their mental processes. Epicurus knew that *the act of creation stabilized his soul; what could have been a more pleasurable experience* for this most intellectual of all human beings?

Epicurus composed over 300 philosophical works, which places him beyond the realm of most mere mortals. Nevertheless, as is the case in extreme situations, the lesson to be learned is more obvious than in ordinary situations. *Creative expression forms the soul.* In case a reader may wonder why it necessary to indulge in antiquarianism to demonstrate the thesis, I shall resist the answer that the men of antiquity, *kata syneidēsin,* were in many ways superior to the men of today. It is possible to obtain convincing support from that most contemporary of modern thinkers, Søren Kierkegaard, who in independence of mind and prolific writings might easily be compared to Epicurus. In one of Kierkegaard's many confessions, we find the following statement (discussed in Chapter 10 but deserving of repetition):

> 'Before God', religiously, when I talk with myself, I call of the whole literary activity [of S.K.] my own upbringing and development...

Now what is more pleasurable than developing and bringing up one's own self or, what is the same thing, forming one's soul? The epicurean joys of palate and eros (which Epicurus placed beneath intellectual joys) are hardly comparable after the first few dips into the pond of spiritual *hedonē*. Of course, I assume I am speaking to those who have put away childish things as recommended by the apostle Paul—or at least are not enslaved by them—because children cannot be expected to be concerned with souls.

St. Augustine, in his calling as a philosopher, has said that there are only two questions for philosophy, God and the soul; but I have narrowed this list to one, the soul. God is a subject people should be cautious in philosophizing about, including those (perhaps especially those) who speak *ex cathedra*. The soul, however, can be discussed *ex cathedra* by anyone whose interior self has developed into a certain level of consciousness; one does not have to be a priest or professor to be aware of one's soul. Furthermore, there is a remarkable phenomenon pertaining to the soul; namely, the more one searches into it, the more it grows. It is much like Pinocchio's nose, except that truth instead of falsehood is the growth-enhancing stimulus. It is to be expected that there will be cynics reviving Pilate's response to this kind of talk—Nietzsche believed Pilate's question "What is truth?" to be the only worthwhile line in all the Greek scriptures—but cynics have always existed and will always exist in all ages. One's heart is where one's treasure is.

This writing then is about the existence of the soul. It is not a scholarly treatise, thus there is no accompanying scholarly apparatus, e.g. references, notes, bibliography, etc. The principal justification for the work to me is that I have developed myself through its writing. I would like to make it available to those who have an interest in this topic, albeit one cannot be sanguine about such interest in this most materialist of eras. Still, *habent sua fata libelli;* writings, like people, have their fate that no one can predict. I know I would have liked to encounter this book if it had been authored by another. Perhaps in some future time, when my fires of literary expression have been extinguished and this writing will in fact appear to have been written by another, I will come upon it and recall a state of mind in which I could have echoed the thought of Teilhard de Chardin about his own writings:

J'expose avant tout des vues ardentes.

---

*Kata syneidēsin—according to reflective or higher consciousness. An ancient Greek expression found throughout the pages of this work. The term has the merit of meaning both reflective consciousness and conscience, thus bringing together what is artificially separated in English. This separation does not occur in most other European languages.

1. The Soul Exists

THE IDEA OF THE 'soul' is not in high standing today as a subject of serious discussion. The word itself is suspect, evoking images of religious superstitions or poetic license. It may be acceptable for professional clergy to speak of souls because of longstanding traditions of religious rhetoric, but otherwise it is not really a meaningful expression in a scientifically oriented society. In modern literature, the term *soul* is a figure of speech, so to speak—a literary device by which the writer acknowledges qualities of personality or character. Reference to the soul of an individual is intended to have the same meaning as reference to the soul of a nation or of a people in which a literary abstraction replaces literal meaning. It is understood that an individual does not have a soul in the way he has limbs or viscera or a brain.

It was not always so in western societies. Perhaps there has been no greater transformation of the western worldview than in the conception of the soul, which formerly was the chief concept that distinguished Christians from heathens. Whether one regards this change as enlightened progressiveness or descent into blasphemy, its impact on the mental outlook of individuals can hardly be denied. The faith of a materia-oriented society centers on the belief that reality consists of physical being—all else is either wishful thinking or metaphysical dreaming. If belief in God remains widespread for reasons of tradition and psychology, there are generally no further concessions among the educated segment of the population to the unseen and unseeable. Angels, demons and assorted spirits, which were once firmly believed to populate the world along with plants and animals, have now largely been consigned to the dust heap of discarded superstitions. And, though modified by a decent respect for religious sensibilities, so has the belief in the existence of a 'metaphysical soul.'

Although the materialist worldview precludes belief in the soul as an existent reality, certain contradictory features can be noted in the attitudes of those who otherwise live by this view. Developed individuals, no matter how dominated they are by object-oriented materialism in their daily lives, yearn for the qualities of being that are associated with the concept of a soul. They want to possess individual autonomy, which is no more than saying they do not want to be the stimulus-response beings required by materialist psychology. They are not content existing as cogs in the mechanisms of society; they want to have depth, scope and values in their lives, however they may conceive these soul-related concepts. The developed individuals of either sex want to rise above instinctual drives, meaning they want to transcend biology. In short, they want to live *as if* they have souls that need expression. The remarkable survival of religious institutions in materialist societies is a testimonial to this desire for spiritual, i.e. soul-related, existence.

Whatever residual acceptance of the idea of a soul remains in western culture is largely based upon Christian beliefs that provide its chief religious tradition. These beliefs teach that God in his many manifestations and infinite mercy is the saving support of the human soul for those favored by His presence. Without divine mediation, Christian doctrine simply does not permit any significant development of a soul. The idea of God and the idea of the human soul are inextricably merged in Christian spiritual thought. Thus the doctrine of *grace* becomes necessary concerning the soul since it is unthinkable that an individual by himself could obtain the divine presence. A certain respect for consistency must be accorded to the Calvinist tenet of predestination.

However, we do not live in a time in which much reliance is placed upon divine grace; other than by professional clergymen. Several centuries ago during the renaissance of philosophy as an *independent* form of thought, René Descartes observed that anyone interested in reality should abandon all preconceptions and start afresh, using his mature rational faculties to make a new start in constructing a worldview. This is excellent advice for anyone wishing to discover his own soul as well as to explore the concept of the soul as a unique phenomenon occurring in the human species. It is a purifying exercise to abandon dogmas that are instilled in one's mind before one is capable of thinking independently. One may then begin to confront the uniquely human problem of existence.

Reasons for the decline of belief in the soul are not hard to find. The prevailing scientific-material worldview has little in common with the goal of antique philosophy to apprehend the realities of existence as opposed to mythological constructs. We live in an era in which human mental powers are exclusively devoted toward control of the physical universe. Science is no longer rational, it is mechanical and dependent on a gigantic technology that it has evolved. Like the ancient dinosaurs, it is materia-bound by its instrumental armor. The modern scientist is a career-oriented professional specialist who has no inclination to address himself to a way of thought that is not materia-based. Yet it is the scientists who provide the prevailing model of reality for society.

The construction of a 'creative nihilism' in the mind with respect to the soul quickly reveals that there is very little in contemporary culture to support the idea of a soul. There are many formulas for success and happiness in our society but none for acquiring a soul. Superannuated scriptural rhetoric or creedal traditions cannot be relied upon. One must begin afresh, just as Descartes suggested, relying only on one's own experiences and mental abilities.

The primary datum for belief in one's soul comes from the individual reflecting on his own nature. No developed personality whose mind has not been dulled by the habit of concrete thinking can doubt the existence of his consciousness. A higher consciousness is part of what is meant by the word soul. The soul is more than physiological wakefulness, memory or mental processing; it is the unique metaphysical state of mind that exists in humans. To deny the soul is to deny the self.

The ensemble of conscious emotions, volitions and ideas, active and latent, is what forms the soul. It is absurd to deny its existence; it is like denying the existence of one's body. The more of these elements a person has, the more soul he has. One is not born with a soul; it is acquired. Those individuals whose consciousness is limited to certain areas are persons with limited souls. The person with a broad range of consciousness, deep in intelligence as well as varied in scope, containing the full complement of human capacities, is someone with a richly endowed soul. The men of Greek antiquity called such a person a *Sophos*, a man of wisdom. More than recognizing this person, they valued him and regarded the acquisition of a higher consciousness as the principal purpose of human endeavor.

The soul is not subject to physical analysis, therefore one cannot consider it a form of matter with properties of force, weight or extension. This does not mean it is not real since there is no justifiable reason to give scientific materialism a monopoly on the entire realm of reality. It is as much a real phenomenon as any law of gravity or thermodynamics. No human concept—and the laws of nature assuredly fall into this category—can be relied upon to give a complete picture of reality. For a substance to be regarded as real, scientific materialism requires it to be amenable to physical analysis. But what if the soul is metaphysical and not subject to the laws of energy and matter? The techniques of science would then be of no value in evaluating it.

The claim of the soul to reality is not based on weights and measures, it is based on the awareness of self in *Homo sapiens.* All higher activities of human beings are founded upon the cultivation of consciousness—art, literature, music, religion; all of these strive to elevate consciousness. Without a higher consciousness, i.e. without a soul, one does not fully qualify as a human being and the mark of brutishness throughout the ages has not been the absence of freedom, it has been the absence of a higher consciousness. To repeat what has been said earlier, questioning the reality of the soul is absurd, it is like questioning the reality of self. It is a denial of the essential human characteristic. There is no evidence, however, that one is endowed with a soul at birth; one must have a commitment to the development of self.

Consciousness can also be made the subject of methodological study, such as has been done by professors of philosophy, especially in the German-speaking world of scholarship. Hegel and Husserl are notable figures in the evolution of the science of consciousness. Edmund Husserl singlehandedly produced a whole new branch of philosophical 'science' known as *phenomenology*. Producing a science of consciousness, however, is not the same as possessing a higher consciousness. Husserl, like Hegel, was a university professor concerned with establishing the study of consciousness and mind as a scholarly activity. This is the current approach of university analytic philosophy. Husserl avoided treading on the toes of the religious and cultural authorities of their day and identified with scientism, instead of perceiving how profoundly antithetical modern science was to notions of consciousness. Some philosophers have had the totally unrealistic idea that philosophy was the "queen" of the sciences; whereas the fact is that they are no more noticed by professional scientists than are the janitors in their laboratories. (One might safely wager that most scientists would rate the latter as more important than philosophers.) One should not be deceived by a few scientists who have philosophical interests outside of their scientific work into thinking that contemporary science looks to philosophy for anything of relevance.

The most unfortunate aspect of the materialist worldview is that it ignores spiritual reality, the reality of the soul. This rejection is pervasive in the mentality of the times, even among ostensibly religious individuals. The scientifically-minded person through early education and constant reinforcement does not truly relate to anything not accessible to the senses or to the instruments developed to enlarge sensory capacities. This is an irrational attitude, one indicative of the arrogance of the scientific mentality since there is no reason to believe that the five senses provide exclusive access to every element of existence. The evidence of an incorporeal soul is not based on spiritual tricks or parlor games, but upon the evidence of self-awareness and the phenomena of culture in human history. Science cannot explain this awareness and these phenomena on materialistic terms. To regard them as epiphenomena of neuronal discharges is like thinking the music of a Chopin to be due to the depression of the keys of the piano upon which Chopin played.

The soul is a 'reality' that is incorporeal. This is the alpha and omega of consciousness of the nature of self. The soul participating in a living body forms the human *Existenz* as distinguished from a soulless mammal walking on two feet. The contemporary independent philosopher D.R. Khashaba defines the soul as "the enduring locus of the creative activity that is all the reality we know" (*Quest of Reality*). The fact that one cannot express the soul in familiar mechanistic formulae has nothing to do with its reality. Exclusive monism is the simplistic attitude of the dogmatists of materialism and has led to the principal problem of western society, lack of attention to the soul. Nevertheless, the impulse toward its development persists and leads to serious tensions in individuals who do not acknowledge it. The person who does not attend to his own soul impoverishes it just as surely as lack of attention to any part of the human condition leads to impoverishment of the rejected part.

2. The Human Condition

WE HUMAN BEINGS find ourselves in a vast physical void populating a tiny planet that has no more material significance than does a drop of water in the oceans of the planet. We are on this planet with numerous other life forms with which we share many characteristics. It is notable that no evidence of life has been detected elsewhere in the universe and as the capacity of astronomers to probe the stellar spaces increases without discovering life, the possibility increases that the life on this planet may be unique. The Ptolemaic cosmology in which our planet is at the center of the universe may have been correct from the perspective of biology. It may be that the emergence of life on planet Earth represents some fundamental alteration in the nature of the universe whose *raison d'être* we are not in a position to determine. However, it compares in significance to the cosmic explosion that astronomers say was responsible for the current ensemble of planetary bodies. No amount of laboratory gene play alters the fact that animate being is fundamentally different from inanimate being. The laws of physics govern the material universe; the laws of biology govern life.

The appearance of life has not been the last word in the destiny of planet Earth. A change as fully significant as the appearance of life has emerged as *consciousness* in the human life form. Consciousness is as dramatic a change in the nature of existence as was the cosmic explosion or the emergence of life. We who are conscious are as different from unconscious life as it is from inanimate bodies. While there may be traces of a rudimentary consciousness in other animal forms or even plants, they are a different nature compared to a developed human consciousness. The appearance of human consciousness rivals in import the planetary circuits around the sun. Metaphors for consciousness are difficult to construct because it represents a radically new element in existence.

The evolution of human society is a matter of development of new forms of consciousness. When cavemen began to paint figures on the walls of their dwellings, a new dimension was added to their lives, that of conscious representation of the world in which they lived. There are many kinds of consciousness that form the soul. There is consciousness of self, of family, of race and country, of history and homeland. There is consciousness of emotions, desires, capacities and a linguistic consciousness. The religious consciousness is a notable aspect of the human condition resulting in awareness of a metaphysical dimension of the universe. Finally, there is currently the most influential consciousness, the scientific form in which man develops an understanding of natural laws and learns to control nature. Consciousness is ever changing, enlarging and contracting, intensifying and diminishing, tinged by emotion, driven by desire and delineated by thought. To repeat a theme of the previous chapter, *soul* is the word utilized to refer to the entire ensemble of latent and active consciousness of an individual. Its coming into being is the manifest goal of human development.

The soul is not a transient abstraction; it is a durable feature of the personality of an individual. Because it *is* incorporeal, it is not easily related to the objects of material existence. The materialist worldview does not recognize incorporeal substance as real so that discussions about the soul have an unreal quality to the materia-oriented person. But the soul is very real in human life. When one is attuned to the significance of the incorporeal soul, it is intensely real and the most absorbing of all subjects that come to human attention.

Human beings begin this life as raw unconscious creatures, reflexively kicking and screaming in their struggle to survive life *extra utero*. The instinctual parts of the personality dominate the early years of life. But very soon, humans begin to deviate from other animal species in their never ending search for consciousness. The urge to develop a soul is as powerful a drive as is any animal instinct.

Children want to explore the world, master their environment and relate to other living creatures. Motor skills develop with astonishing rapidity. The drive to acquire language skills; to understand, speak and read is universal in all societies not mired in primitiveness. Speech and literacy are vehicles for expanding consciousness since the written word is a remarkable telescope permitting the reader to experience the consciousness of other times and other places. It is only the crudest of societies that justify literacy on utilitarian grounds without acknowledging the principal purpose of reading in humans—transmission of cultural consciousness. As children mature into adult life, the desire to explore the world and the people within it intensifies. This is a normal function of the lifelong drive toward creation of one's soul. Even the scientific study of the physical world was initially a manifestation of this *need to know*, although it has been now largely covered over by utilitarian considerations.

Consciousness is what is new in the universe. What is especially new is that a human being is not merely conscious of his surroundings, he is also conscious of his interior self. Consciousness reflecting on itself is like an individual unexpectedly coming upon an entrance to a cave in the basement of his little home, a cave that has an infinite number of passageways if one has the fortitude to explore its depths:

> The limits of the soul cannot be found though you would travel over it every way, so deep is its logos.
>
> -- Heraclitus

This saying, stemming from the dawn of Greek philosophy, previews the attitude of the Greek philosophers of antiquity who recognized human consciousness as the epitome of human evolution. The Greeks did not merely recognize the value of consciousness, they adapted their lives to it so as to promote its development. No virtue was more important than development of the soul; the principal requirement of this development was interior exploration. The *gnōthi seauton*—know thyself—on the wall of Delphi did not refer only to an understanding of repressed drives in the Freudian sense, it referred principally to an awareness of self as a definite entity whose first principle was the cultivation of consciousness. All other goals for the philosopher were subordinated to this first principle of their lives. The extreme posture of the ancient Cynic, and to some degree Stoic, attitudes can only be understood as deriving from devotion to the development of their souls.

Upon this devotion of the philosophers of the antique world came to be superimposed the ideals of Christianity. No matter how one views Christian dogmas, there is no question that consciousness of the soul underlies Christian faith. The preoccupation with soul in post-Roman European history derived from the influence of Christian beliefs. However, today the dominance of the Christian worldview has long passed away.

Now we live in an age of science (some call it the age of money) where religious concepts are tolerated but rarely accorded the dedication given to the world of material objects. The contemporary worldview accords reality only to the realm of existence with physical dimensions; thoughts about incorporeal entities are not taken seriously. At the frontiers of physics, there may be some uncertainty about the exact nature of physical existence, but this ambiguity has not extended into popular thinking where reality is still regarded as something subject to measurement and the laws of physics. It is the stubbornness of this view that has led to the absurd idea that the reality of consciousness is in some way reducible to the activity of brain cells and that the soul is merely a romantic way of referring to higher cortical functions. Its study becomes a matter of analyzing stimulus-response behavior of higher mammals.

All this might be viewed as the province of the professional philosopher or historian whose vocation it is to analyze worldviews. However, one's worldview is not an academic matter, it is the very substance of the life of the individual, determining his relationship with the world around him and generating the motivations for all his activities. A person with a predominantly materialist worldview lives a different life compared to one with a spiritual worldview. The bourgeois lifestyle differs from the monastic lifestyle. Antiquity recognized that the difference between the life of Diogenes the beggar-philosopher and Alexander the Great King was a question of worldview; their contemporaries noted the similarities in each other's temperaments and abilities. All people want to partake of reality but it is their worldview that determines where they think this reality is to be found.

The philosophic term *naive realism* refers to a propensity to believe that reality lies exclusively in tangible matter and that what cannot be measured does not exist. Those who believe only in physical reality are called *naive* because this is the attitude of children who take seriously only what they can touch, see or hear. The reliance on external modalities of perception for a definition of reality excludes the realm of consciousness (the soul) while still depending on consciousness for that which characterizes human life. Even science is founded on consciousness—demonstrated every time primitive people are encountered who have not developed the consciousness required for technological projects. Envisioning the consciousness that produces technology to be itself a byproduct of neuronal 'technology' is a nonsensical point of view. Few thoughtful scientists really believe such an improbable idea, yet so rigid is the scientific-material worldview that the idea of the reality of incorporeal consciousness is mentally repressed as incongruent with modern thought.

Our contemporary world is structured on the belief that physical nature alone is real and that the soul is an illusory epiphenomenon, secondary to human life rather than the essence of it. It leads to values, work habits, educational activities and even pleasures constructed on the premise that real life requires nurturing of the physical self and mastery of the physical environment. The development of mental qualities is directed toward acquisition of skills needed for functioning 'successfully' (i.e. financially) in society. Individuals may have hobbies or interests to occupy leisure time but these are secondary to the business of living in the 'real' material world. There is at most token acceptance of the notion of the soul, which must be placated in order to be happy, but none at all to the idea that the soul represents the essential element of the human condition, which requires effort for its development. For all essential purposes, this attitude disappeared in America with the demise of the Puritan way of thought. Whatever their limitations in other ways, the Puritans took the concept of soul seriously in every aspect of their lives. Such a mentality does not exist today. Contemporary society values the material aspects of existence; e.g. consumerism, careerism and physical health. Culture is directed toward leisure time activities, largely of a passive nature. Enjoyment rather than enlightenment is the characteristic cultural value of our times.

All this would be perfectly logical if reality consisted exclusively of the physical self and other physical phenomena. However, that this is not the case can be easily discovered by anyone who reflects on his own subjective nature. The difference between consciousness and the world of materia is evident. It is not natural awareness that is the problem; it is the culturally-determined worldview that assigns reality only to the physical world. In antiquity, the failure to recognize the realm of consciousness and to accord it the highest place in human affairs was characterized as *barbarianism*. To Zeno and Epicurus, two preeminent models of antique Greek culture, a society such as ours would be regarded, *ipso facto*, as barbaric.

A favorite method of dealing with the question of consciousness by adherents of the material worldview is to refer it to the brain. Somehow it is felt that by connecting consciousness to the brain, the specter of an incorporeal soul will finally be dissipated. Since death of the human organism appears to be associated with the disappearance of human consciousness, this approach is assumed to solve the problem of multiple realities. It is easier to study brain functions than the development of the soul. But one does not evaluate the stage carpentry of Elizabethan days in order to grasp the dramatic artistry of Shakespeare. No appeals to the right, left, or middle brains, no neuroadjectival proliferation—neurolinguistic, neuropsychological, even neurophilosophical (a term recently coined by some misguided academic)—will contribute the slightest bit to the flowering of consciousness and formation of the soul. Reality must be dealt with on its own terms and within its own dimensions. The 'great-souled' individuals of all times, including our own, became so by enlarging their consciousness of spiritual reality. Reflections on experience, contact with other souls and freeing oneself from culture barriers may contribute to this process, although not completely create it. The outstanding flaw of a materialist society is that it does not recognize the human condition as the effort to create a soul.

The development of consciousness is the human activity *par excellence*. One ought to subordinate all other adult activities to this goal. Developing consciousness establishes a person where he ought to be, within a person-centered cosmos. Merely preserving and propagating life equates an individual with a host of other animal species, many of which are much better suited for the competitive business of species survival. But the creation of a human soul is an important metaphysical event standing outside the space-time dimension of physical existence.

3. The Question of Reality

SERIOUS PEOPLE ARE COMMITTED to the idea of reality. They want their lives to be bound up with what is real instead of what is illusory. Except for those treating psychosis, they are not interested in illusory phenomena since these do not possess the attribute of reality. A medieval proof of the existence of God stated that since He was the most perfect being, He must possess the attribute of reality. Lack of reality is one of the most damning of imperfections and although this particular proof of God's existence is based on a logical fallacy, it does emphasize the importance of reality as a concept and value judgment in people's minds.

Perhaps it seems unnecessary to assert that reality is more important than unreality. Everyone knows that they prefer actual possessions to imaginary ones, actual accomplishments to fantasized ones and real friends to false or imaginary ones. The essence of schizophrenia is the choice of an imaginary world over a real one.

Reality is what is universally respected and the 'real world' is a world most people prefer to live in—if they can.

The difficulty with reality lies in the fact that judgments about its presence are based upon phenomena that have as much to do with the perceptions and mindset of the judging person as with the nature of the presumed 'reality.' This insight was Immanuel Kant's enduring contribution to human knowledge. When Samuel Johnson made his celebrated judgment upon the reality of a rock in front of him by kicking it with his gouty great toe, he judged its reality on the basis of the pain induced in his inflamed toe by the shock of the contact. Had the rock been made of papier-mâché, Johnson might have come to a different conclusion. Setting aside the sensitivities of tender toes, it is abundantly evident today that the reality of ordinary objects for casual observers is quite different from that of instrument-laden scientists who are able to vastly extend the limits of normal perceptions. When one extends the concept of reality into more abstract areas, the subjectivity of the judgments is greatly increased. Physics is no more 'real' than metaphysics; it is merely that its observations are more standardized and amenable to predictable judgments. But predictability and standardization are no criteria for reality. The poetry of Shelley with its passion, imagery and intelligence has an intense impact on connoisseurs of English poetry, but might have been dismissed by Henry Ford as lacking in reality. In America, the real world generally has to do with the preoccupations of

Homo economicus. However, the real world of Ford would have had little meaning for Socrates or St. Francis.

Reality for an individual is greatly involved with the particular role he may play in society. For the *paterfamilias*, reality is the cash flow that pays the bills for his family. Reality for the successful author is the number of books sold, with ensuing royalties, prizes, invitations, etc. Politicians judge reality according to the number of votes garnered on election day; revolutionaries prefer the realities of firearms in the hands of their adherents. A plumber judges his realities by the efficiency of keeping subterranean wastes flowing freely without leakage. And so on and so forth. Reality stems from the perceptual functions and value systems of the individual. *Reality is a concept, not a given existent.*

This thought leads to the question of whether there is a universal human reality—aside from the realities perceived by an unencumbered individual, a scientist, a business executive, a congressman, a plumber or a revolutionary fighter. Is there a reality related to humanness *per se* instead of to the innumerable roles people adopt in the course of adapting to and dominating nature? Is there an *objective* reality of universal human value and adaptable to all human beings?

We humans share a great many features with other living creatures. We are born, live, eat and reproduce ourselves. We have developed remarkable technologies for supporting our physical being and for the rearing of our young. We have evolved methods for entertaining ourselves that are truly fantastic. In all of these things, we do not differ in kind from other creatures who also live, eat, reproduce, raise their young and entertain themselves. We live in the same world that they do, which we conceive of as *reality.* What is unique to humans, however, is the appearance of their souls. Descartes defined a human being as a *res cogitans,* a thinking thing, which is as good a definition as any, with the proviso that the thinking refers to interior consciousness, not the manipulative cleverness in which thinking is used like an accessory hand. It is in interior consciousness that the essential quality of humanness resides, and it is in the maximal dimensions of this consciousness that the maximal reality of humans can be found.

For a person not ground down by his society, the highest reality consists in the elaboration of his consciousness. This is the real world for a human being. Therefore, the individual who is committed to reality will strive with all his or her might to endow this consciousness with clarity, variety and intensity. There is nothing he will not do for it consistent with his conscience—which is in itself a form of consciousness. His education will be a matter of filling out its dimensions, his deepest feelings will be connected with its substance and his energies will be devoted toward preserving it from the brutal attacks of society. In short, he will be committed to his own soul as the ultimate reality for him and will spare no efforts in sustaining its integrity. *Homo sapiens* only really loves ideas; toward other individuals, affection is the appropriate emotion.

The creation of a soul demands directing attention inward toward consciousness of interiority. There are no two individuals with identical needs in this area. No one should be so presumptuous as to provide formulae for another. Some will need periods of societal idolatry, infatuation with others or merging with nature. Ultimately, however, it is the interior self that must emerge to form the soul. The real world for humans is the world of the soul.

4. God, Soul and Søren Kierkegaard

A WORLDVIEW IN WHICH the soul is the first order of reality for individuals cannot evade the problem of God for very long. For two millennia, the idea of soul has been intimately associated with belief in a personal God. For the philosophers of Europe up until the eighteenth century, the microcosmic soul was always contrasted with the macrocosmic Deity. In Christian belief, faith in an all powerful God and awareness of the soul yearning for his presence were complementary ideas joined together like love and hate or space and time. When St. Augustine wrote that there were only two questions for philosophy, the soul and God, he stamped an indelible imprint on western thought. It has been said that all philosophy is a footnote to Plato, but the expression might have been better applied to the voluminous writings of Augustine.

However, belief in God and the concept of soul do not emanate from the same source. Awareness of the soul is a primary datum of experience originating in the self. A thinking person cannot disbelieve in his soul, he can only choose to call it by a different name or perhaps ignore it entirely. *Cogito ergo sum* means that consciousness of thought requires a vehicle containing the consciousness. One can no more deny the soul than he can deny the visible physical self. He may, impelled by the monism of a materialist worldview, be inclined to think his soul is a manifestation of his physical self but this is not denying the soul, it is merely choosing to bring together two entirely separate dimensions of existence, an approach warned against by Aristotle. One might say that life is desoxyribonucleic acid but all know that the phenomenon of life is much more than a simple chemical substance.

Belief in God is quite another matter. Except for those few mystics who claim direct communication from Him, belief in God is a matter of *faith*, faith that may stem from various sources. For the vast majority of people, faith in God is something they absorb from their society in the same way that they wear clothes in public or eat with utensils. It is an aspect of their culture that they accept *in good faith* without any need to validate this faith. After a time, belief in God becomes second nature—a habit of mind analogous to locking the door when one leaves the home. There is not the constant reinforcement of direct experience that underlies the intuitive knowledge of the soul. Even the most fervent mystic has only rare direct 'experiences' of God to reinforce his commitment to the belief.

Most individuals believe in God because they cannot imagine that there should not be a God.

The 'proofs' of God's existence lie in the apparent necessity of the belief; i.e., the contradictory belief is inconceivable. There must be a first cause, a Creator for the created things in universe. *Natura naturata* must have its *Natura naturans,* which is the almighty world power. This feeling that has been so recurrent in human mental history deserves considerable attention, as does any constantly recurring human attitude. The ancient Greeks and Romans were subject to the same feeling; however, they rarely imagined that they were privy to the detailed thoughts or wishes of a supreme deity. Such a claim was ludicrous or blasphemous, which is how the educated classes of Mediterranean antiquity regarded the early Christians. One can make many statements about the soul from direct experience; very little can be said about a supreme deity from similar sources. If a deity exists, he is truly a *Deus absconditus,* a hidden god, and the appropriate theology is a *negative theology* that does not attribute to him any qualities conceived by humans. This is an old idea within theological circles.

For devout Christians, however, God is revealed through the mind of Jesus Christ and Christian sects have evolved numerous dogmas claiming to be founded on the divine will. It is this *positive theology* that fell afoul of the Enlightenment in Europe and led to the great weakening of the spiritual impulse in European culture. How could teachings claiming to be God's will compare with the certainty of the laws of physics? The dubious legends and puny miracles of a procession of Christian saints could hardly measure up to the accomplishments of modern science and industry. Belief in God might be embedded in European culture but it could not compete with electric power and the internal combustion engine. A spiritual worldview based on an unknown, unexperienced deity gave way before the overwhelming impact of scientific technology. Individuals could still *confess* a faith in their religion but all their energies went in a different direction. Heinrich Heine was perhaps the first to suggest that God was 'sick'; afterwards, his 'death' was bluntly noted by Nietzsche. These were the metaphors of insightful thinkers orienting themselves to the new realities of the times. It was hardly noted at first that along with the death of God, the disappearance of the soul was also occurring.

It may be that the psychology of human being requires a viable concept of a macrocosm in order to sustain a microcosmic consciousness. Belief in God may really represent the "charter of liberty" for the individual as Nikolai Berdyaev often wrote. However, while all the content of the soul derives from human experience, belief in God is based upon the consciousness of limitations of self. The great unknown lying beyond human capacities is what gives rise to this belief. This is how one understands the negative theology mentioned earlier that has had a modest place in Christian theology. There is no more dangerous manifestation of hubris in an individual than to think that he knows more than he does. Consciousness of ignorance, not fear of God, is the beginning of wisdom; wise souls who come to the realization that there is a vast domain of being that they do not know and cannot know call this domain 'God.' The moment one begins to imagine that there is a positive content to this consciousness—whether it stems from purported revelation or superior wisdom—the proper consciousness of God is distorted. It should be awareness that the human soul is limited in its capabilities, not superior in wisdom, that leads to a belief in God. This belief is of a different nature than that derived from experience but perhaps is not thereby less significant.

The justification of faith in a metaphysical deity is dependent on the content of the faith. If one believes in a God judging sinners and rewarding the good, than very little believability can be accorded to such a faith. The basis of this faith was clearly expounded by Ludwig Feuerbach (*Essence of Christianity*) who recognized the psychological mechanism of *projection* in the usual portrayal of God. A loving, benevolent, demanding, punishing, rewarding God is palpably an imaginary being endowed with the full range of human emotions. The predisposition of individuals to project their feelings onto other creatures was defined by Freud and is not a matter of dispute among those familiar with mental processes. There is no reason to endow a supreme deity with human qualities other than the human tendency to project his own feelings onto others. However, if one regards the concept of God as an acknowledgement that reality extends beyond the scope of human consciousness, then a faith in God is justified, even necessary. A God that dwells beyond the human purview may be the only God that exists.

One notes that determined atheists are found among those who do not recognize their own limitations in awareness of reality. Scientists are predisposed to this tendency. Narcissistically inclined individuals are also predisposed since they are self-centered on visible realities. On the other hand, a religious consciousness encourages awareness of God because it recognizes existence of metaphysical dimensions of reality. But this awareness in Christianity has often not been founded on a genuine humility and has introduced all kinds of 'positive theology' based on personal projections and prejudices.

What if in the evolution of life—that improbable phenomenon appearing in our tiny corner of the physical universe—there has been a sudden change in direction of this evolution, a change from life moving outward to moving inward and thereby changing its nature? What if the unknown God has 'decided' (an admitted projection) that instead of spreading over and subduing his surroundings, *Homo sapiens* shall now enter into the metaphysical domain of consciousness? What if the moving hand of destiny shall now enter into human souls causing every individual to be compelled to seek out the limits of his own soul? What if the kingdom to come will be a kingdom within the self instead of a kingdom without? Perhaps the Arbiter of being has indeed ordained that the kingdom of heaven is within the soul and all else for humans is irrelevant or unapproachable. As Socrates once cleverly asserted (according to Plato), it would not be fitting for a sensible person to insist that all this will be just as described, but that this or something like it may have truth to it is worthy of consideration and even of faith.

Initially, the soul's departure along with God seemed to be good riddance to old rubbish. Just as the mathematician Laplace had no need of God in his system of astronomy, so the behavioral psychologists have no need of the soul in their stimulus-response psychology. Rudolf Virchow after dissecting a thousand brains is said to have remarked that he had never once come across a soul. The story may be apocryphal but it is indicative of the temper of the times. The doctrine of scientific materialism promised constant progress; ideas encumbered with incorporeal souls were embarrassments, reeking of medievalism, superstition and ecclesiastical tyrannies. All that people needed was the intelligence to deal with nature and the will to apply their abilities. Progress was inevitable once one had the hang of positive thought and knew how to use it to good purpose. A 'developed' individual was no longer one who knew the classical languages and possessed the cultural wherewithal implied by the mastery of the classics; he was now a person with a profession, ability to make money and a recognized position in society. A 'developed' nation was one that was advanced industrially; undeveloped nations were ones that were not—

period. No other factors counted except material performance in materially acquisitive societies.

Human beings may be able to get along superficially without a belief in God, but to get along without consciousness of their soul has turned out to be another matter. The ignoring of the soul has led to the spread of *Angst,* which has been noted by acute observers with a sufficient consciousness of the deeper needs of the human condition. In the best of times in American history, Henry David Thoreau observed that most men—to say nothing of women—lived lives of quiet desperation. Perhaps Thoreau dealt in literary hyperbole, but he never wrote a word that did not reveal an underlying truth.

The name of Søren Kierkegaard is unalterably affixed to the statement that "truth is subjectivity," which is just a terse way of saying that one's soul is the most important aspect of his existence. Now Kierkegaard has quite a bit more to say on the subject as anyone who has made the effort to read his works can well attest. In his *Concluding Unscientific Postscript,* Kierkegaard's magnum opus, he makes the humorous little confession that when he began his authorship, he decided after reviewing his own peculiar capabilities that "You [S.K.] must do something, but inasmuch with your limited capacities, it will be impossible to make anything easier…you must with the same humanitarian enthusiasm as the others, undertake to make it harder." It is in this spirit that we should understand Kierkegaard's use of the term 'Christianity' to refer to the unique philosophy that he set forth. Even though he makes it quite clear that his point of view has nothing in common with what he calls "objective, doctrinal, childish Christianity" and that he renounces what Christendom has understood Christianity to be, he still stubbornly continues to make his allegiance to Christianity (although he declines to presume he himself has achieved the Christian state). Like the fruitless search of the ancient Stoics for a man of ideal virtue, Kierkegaard was never able to find or become a perfect Christian.

Kierkegaard in his writings may be taken at his word that he desired to make things more difficult. He obscured his "existential communication" by calling it an ideal Christianity, while in fact it had nothing to do with existent Christianity. Instead of Christianity, he might have called his beliefs 'Inwardism' or 'Subjectivism' or 'Kierkegaardism.' If he wished to acknowledge his precursors, he might have coined the term 'Neochristianism' or perhaps more accurately, 'Neoneoplatonism.' Things would have been clearer conceptually, even if more awkward semantically. However, true to his resolution, he made things more difficult for his readers.

Nevertheless, Kierkegaard is entitled to his eccentricities. He was the first person to develop the religious impulse into a truly profound philosophy, instead of congealing it into sectarianism. Kierkegaard understood that, at the core of human existence, the religious impulse and the self-actualizing impulse are identical. He maintained that the essence of this impulse was a turning within instead of staying without, with one or another 'doctrine.' The development of his soul was Kierkegaard's religion, whatever allusions he might make to historical Christianity. He expropriated Christian metaphysics and made it into a vehicle for his own use; one might add that it became a far more profound and insightful vehicle than it ever was or has been in the hands of theologians.

The nature of reality for the individual has never been more fully and meaningfully expressed than in the prose of Kierkegaard. The new man for him is "the Subjective Thinker who is an Existing Individual, aesthetic enough to give his life aesthetic content, ethical enough to regulate it and dialectical enough to interpenetrate it with thought." Kierkegaardian existence is an art form that few have been able to master.

5. The Impact of Culture

THE CONSCIOUSNESS OF AN individual who has lived all his life on a deserted island differs greatly from one raised amidst the full complement of European culture. This may appear too obvious to need stating but it is often necessary to remind oneself of the circumstantial nature of one's mind. The mindset of Kierkegaard is unimaginable in China as is that of Mao Tsetung in contemporary Denmark. The impact of culture on an individual refers to the multitude of societal influences affecting his development; the problem of culture for the individual is becoming conscious of these influences and subordinating them to his interior self. It is impossible for a person to develop his soul without an awareness of the historical forces acting upon him. This would be like the owner of an automobile trying to repair his vehicle without any idea of how it was manufactured. A great deal of thought is required to come to a consciousness of the impact of one's culture upon one's self. Culture includes not only immediate contemporary influences, but also the ethos of a society that may stretch back for centuries, even millennia. It is relatively easy to assess the effect of parental influences; it requires more thought to come to a consciousness of traditional attitudes extending back in time.

There are many societies that have a poorly developed sense of history. When European explorers and settlers encountered the natives of North America, the latter were incapable of providing reliable historical accounts of their past. Their spiritual traditions, profound though they might have been and comparing favorably with European religions, were founded upon myths and legends transmitted orally without reference to historical individuals. It was one of the many accomplishments of the Greeks of antiquity to develop an historical consciousness and the apparatus for transmission of thought that was later incorporated into European culture. This gave the Greeks a deepened consciousness of their own selves. The preeminence of Greek culture was due in no small measure to the ability of individuals to experience the consciousness of their predecessors.

The historical dominance of Europe in matters of the mind is founded upon the possession of *Geistesgeschichte,* an important concept for which there is, perhaps significantly, no equivalent word in English. *Geistesgeschichte* is the history of ideas that have been important at various times in history. The person who wishes to develop his consciousness must attend to this history rather than to the mechanical chronicling of battles, kingships and empire formation that has so long formed the content of history. Even now, although more attention is paid to everyday existence and class conflicts, there is little in depth explorations of *Geistesgeschichte* in usual historical accounts. One may hear about the *Zeitgeist*, the spirit of the times, but little about the minds of specific persons who may have impacted culture. This approach is a residue of the Hegelian mentality that is of little value to the soul of the existent individual.

The searching soul who wishes to learn about the development of his consciousness gains nothing from impersonal studies of sociology. This does not mean he does not need history of culture, it means he is not getting the history he needs. The interior oriented person is in need of a history of significant individuals whose ideas affected their society and became incorporated into their culture. The attitudes of a society do not appear *de novo*, as if by spontaneous generation, they stem from individuals with powerful ideas and the capacity to imprint them on their surroundings.

Beyond the question of learning about the origin of traditions, there is the matter of the need for significant contact with what the antique Greeks called 'great-souled' individuals. Finding such souls is like looking for water in a desert—there are oases for those who know how to look for them. Societies are redeemed by having preserved the souls of their creative personalities. The preservation of the personality of Socrates and his inspired contemporaries and successors justified the politically collapsing Greek city-states of that era. The brutalities of the Roman Empire have been overshadowed by their literary more than their architectural achievements. Bourgeois Copenhagen was forever ennobled by Kierkegaard, as was Concord by Emerson and Thoreau. All this may be thought of as literary romanticism, but it will not alter the fact that the spiritual development of an individual is greatly enhanced by awareness of great-souled predecessors.

The number of these individuals whose expressions have survived the vicissitudes of time is pitifully small. They are the holy men of civilization whose accessibility is essential for spiritual development. The odd belief of some that God will favor them with spiritual consciousness through access to a particular religious doctrine is not worthy of serious consideration. Spiritual development is strictly an affair of the inner self, the soul, and is stimulated by intimate contact with the souls of spiritually superior individuals. The phenomenon of discipleship is based on such contacts. However, in the climate of our era, genuine discipleship is rare. There are a great many charismatic 'teachers' of spirituality but it is impossible to gain genuine access to the soul of an instructor who is being paid for the contact. One cannot be taught 'how to' achieve a higher self; this is a concept derived from the world of materia. And no matter how idealized, the phenomenon of erotic love is principally founded upon physical rather than spiritual attraction. Our materialistic society is rarely a suitable place for souls to touch each other.

Yet if the soul were not projected into the surrounding world, development of mankind would not be possible; at most it would be a feeble spasmodic kind of development doomed to pointless repetition. Nietzsche seemed to like this idea in his doctrine of "eternal recurrence," but the phenomenon of Nietzsche could not have occurred without the prior cultures of antiquity, Christianity and a century of German philosophical idealism. One can no more develop the soul without the experience of other souls than he could swim the English Channel without prior swimming experience. In view of the uncertainties of spiritual contact, it is unfortunate that concern for its nurturance is left to superannuated religious institutions.

Who among us has the spontaneous creativity and determination that makes contact with other souls unnecessary? Are the recipients of 'grace' so sure of their spiritual wellbeing as to make unnecessary a different kind of spiritual stimulation? Is the body of Christ still really present in our society after two thousand years of waiting for his return? People turn to outworn religious institutions out of a need for spiritual development but perhaps a new approach is necessary. It seems that with the universal epidemics of drugs, alcoholism, obesity, and other hedonistic manias, individuals in contemporary societies are suffering with a lack of spiritual sustenance, a lack so severe that the nature of the human condition is being altered as people try to adapt to the impersonal nature of exclusively materialistic societies.

There is no concern for the state of the soul in society because the concept is meaningless in it. It is meaningless because the materialist worldview prohibits perception of the soul as a reality. There is only belief in the body and the brain, and acceptance of transitory mental states that are the outcome of brain functions. No one believes souls exist because the belief is not consonant with scientific thinking. Instead of evolution of spiritually developed individuals, our society is moving in the direction of the robotization predicted by George Orwell and Aldous Huxley, and visually depicted in the media in recent years.

Nothing is ever accomplished for individuals *en masse*. The individual, whatever his circumstances, must be able to utilize his experiences to lift himself out of the condition of popular inertia. The heroes of antiquity were the independent philosophers who taught themselves spiritual development; they became 'born again' through a rigorous effort of willpower. What the spiritually impoverished masses in America and many other places lack is *consciousness of their soul*; they do not need more technology in an already technologically overburdened age. It was the treason to philosophy of Karl Marx to elevate the reality of economic progress over that of interior development; as such, he is destined one day to be viewed as the philosophic Judas figure of the modern world. No rationalization can justify the betrayal of philosophy to materialism by someone who should have known better.

Robotization of human life is the *Zeitgeist* of the new millennium. But the secret of any *Geist* of history is...that it has no reality in itself. There is really no such thing as societal attitudes, cultural traditions or religious faith; the only genuine metaphysical realities are to be found in individuals trying to find their way in life. The medieval scholastics called this belief *nominalism*, indicating that such abstract terms are only names. This is a healthy reaction to excessive abstract thought. The individual is the ultimate reality—let us pray to be saved from those who have lost sight of this reality. This was the message of Max Stirner whose vision expressed in *Der Einzige und sein Eigentum* was ridiculed not only by the religious establishment but even more savagely by power-hungry ex-philosophers who dreamed of changing the world.

A *Zeitgeist* is always the enemy of individual development; consciousness of it is like sensing the existence of a poison gas in the atmosphere—it is necessary to take measures in order to survive. Witness the difficulty of spiritual interaction in the current 'age of money,' as Berdyaev called our era. All the attitudes and habits of society operate against it. The pressures, problems and trivialities of day-to-day existence crowd out a higher consciousness. Like Herman Melville's hero in *Pierre*, "one can be in his deepest, highest part, utterly without sympathy from anything divine, human, brute or vegetable" and "as solitary as at the Pole" amidst family, friends, colleagues and acquaintances.

In this contemporary era, where existence of the soul is regarded as a superstition, where everyday life beats out the constant refrain, 'only matter is real, only matter is real, only matter is real,' the knowledge that great-souled individuals have existed is a strengthening consciousness. It provides the steel girders upon which to build one's own soul. It is not a question of being aware of the existence of such and such an historical personage. It is becoming aware of his soul through literary experiences. There is little to be gained by knowing that there was an impoverished Athenian philosopher named Antisthenes in the fifth century B.C., that he was said to have been constantly in the company of Socrates, that he wrote a number of long vanished treatises and that he conducted an ongoing feud with Plato. None of these facts have value in developing our own soul. However when we learn that he responded to the question, "What have you gained from philosophy, Antisthenes?" with the answer, "The ability to converse with myself," we are suddenly catapulted into a new level of consciousness. The terse response communicates the soul of Antisthenes. It reveals that the consciousness of the interior self existed millennia ago in an individual living in Athens. It means that Antisthenes had discovered his inner kingdom long before the Palestinian events announcing a similar discovery. The senselessness of history has deprived us of the pleasure of being able to read Antisthenes elaborating on his thought himself, but the response is enough to reveal that Antisthenes had discovered his own soul and held it in higher regard than all the pleasures of the antique world. This knowledge is of inestimable value in solidifying our own consciousness of inner realty.

But there are dangers. Thought processes confined to the interior self without reference to the surrounding world suggests madness (schizophrenia in psychiatric terminology). Madness is a turning away from external reality in which the individual *prefers* illusions to reality. Many of the great-souled individuals of the past were suspected of being mad; some of them thought themselves to be mad. Plato himself (who was definitely not mad) suggested that there was a close relationship between philosophy and madness. Turning into oneself means a turning away from the external world, with the consequent weakening of the 'normal' psychology that sustains existence in the world. History has disclosed that the paradox of spiritual development is that the process endangers physical existence. The crucifixion is the great Christian symbol of this paradox. But even if the world takes no hostile notice, the individual who seeks to develop his soul separates himself from the world, and if he is too impetuous in his efforts, he runs the risk of breakdown, both physical and psychological. The classic example of this tragedy is the case of Friedrich Nietzsche.

Significant contact with the soul of another individual, even indirectly through writings, letters or testimonies, is the saving grace for the person who is absorbed with his own consciousness. If he cannot make such contacts, the effort toward inwardness is hazardous and perhaps better not made. There is rarely a record of a great-souled individual who did not relate to some earlier figure. The personality of the historical Jesus is unimaginable without the examples of the Hebrew prophets to which he constantly referred and upon whom he clearly depended. Socrates was a model figure to the charismatic founders of the Greek schools of philosophy who followed him. All the Christian saints, all the giants of European thought would not have been possible without predecessors who gave them confidence in their sense of interior reality. Spiritual contact with great-souled individuals who exist or who have existed is the *sine qua non* of spiritual development; one cannot ever find anything that will substitute for it. The practical wisdom of Christianity lies in the creation of a symbolic figure that will support the soul. But a real figure is better than a symbolic one. Any writing or other personal expression that genuinely conveys the soul of a real person can be Holy Scripture to another. The problem is to discover the scripture that resonates with one's own consciousness.

Every human being likes to be entertained, diverted, instructed or persuaded at various times in his life, but this is not making contact with the soul of another. There are places for "court jesters and town criers" (Kierkegaard) in every society. But to enter into communion with the soul of another—this is a different matter, a sacred matter. This is the I–Thou relationship that thinkers like Ludwig Feuerbach and Martin Buber perceived to be at the heart of human interactions. This is a matter of experiencing the inner reality of another individual and, conversely, the ability to project one's own inner reality, which has always been the substance of culture throughout history.

6. The Essence of Christianity

THE CHRISTIAN RELIGION DEFINES its purpose to be the saving of souls. It is not demeaning to it to make the analogy with dietetics, which attempts to do for the body what Christianity purports to do for the soul. Everyone is interested in the kind of eating that promotes a sound body; anyone with an awareness of the soul has no less interest in what promotes its existence. However, while the science of dietetics has never been thought essential to obtain adequate dietary nourishment, Christian dogma asserts that its beliefs are the *sole* means of saving the soul. It is widely believed among devout Christians that without Christian faith, the soul is doomed. It is not surprising therefore that those who have lost faith in the Christian religion have also lost belief in the soul.

For individuals living in western societies who are aware of their soul, there are few substitutes for Christian thought. Every aspect of the culture is permeated with Christian influence. No spiritual force in western civilization is as powerful and pervasive as is Christianity. In case one were to have doubts about the truth of this assertion, one need only consider the recent example of Russia where after two generations of official atheism and suppression of religion, Christianity has again come to the fore. It is inevitable that in Communist societies that offer no support for the idea of the soul, the Christian religion provides an irresistible attraction to individuals with spiritual sensibilities.

Christianity is the greatest ideological product of western civilization. No political or economic structures have ever equaled it in human significance. The concept of the importance of the individual as opposed to society is the core feature of Christian belief, more specifically, belief in the individual human soul as the central feature of the human drama. Christianity has fostered the development of interior consciousness in a manner unique in world history. The antique philosophers were pioneers in individual development but it was the Christ-intoxicated preachers and writers who were capable of disseminating their faith throughout all layers of the civilized world. The details of this faith were not its main feature, what was important was the belief in an inner self that could be developed and preserved.

This concept of the inner self was announced by Jesus with the statement "the kingdom of heaven is within you." There is no more important assertion in the New Testament. This idea was enlarged and intensified by the early Christian fathers. There are many of these founders one could mention; Clement of Alexandria, adapter of antique philosophy to Christian faith, the imaginative Origen, the Cappadocian fathers, Basil and the two Gregorys, and finally, the greatest antique exponent of interior consciousness, Augustine. Little is to be gained by emphasizing the doctrinal squabbles and recriminations of those times; what stands out and is worthy of emphasis is the commitment to inwardness that distinguished early Christianity from the cults and philosophies of the times (perhaps excepting the lonely genius of metaphysics, Plotinus, whose influence could not contend with organized Christianity).

It was perhaps inevitable that the emphasis on the interior self would wane when the Roman Catholic Church replaced the Roman Empire as the unifying *institution* of the western world. But this feature of Christianity was again brought to the forefront by Martin Luther and the leaders of Protestantism who revived Christianity as a religion of interior consciousness. Again, there is no need to emphasize intolerance and bibliolatry in the history of Protestantism; what is important is the renewal of inwardness as central to human existence. One may consider that Protestantism reached its apogee in the figure of Søren Kierkegaard who pushed Christianity to its furthest possible extent as a means of spiritual development.

The concepts of Christian love, sin, guilt and repentance are uniquely Christian ideas representing the centrality of the soul in human existence. These concepts lead to consciousness of inwardness as opposed to the externality that characterized pagan societies. One may make the following assertions to clarify the discussion: *Sin* is the continuous outward direction of human energies no matter how well meaning the motive; *Guilt* is the consciousness of this wrong direction; *Repentance* is the turning away from the material world; and finally, and most importantly, *Love* is the unconditional feeling for one's God. Exception might be taken to these formulations by Christians who would like to give credit to 'good works', but the scriptural message that the just shall live by faith alone seems quite clear. It is the merit of Christianity that it recognized the radically different nature of the message of Jesus—kindness to others had long been part of Jewish teaching—which called the individual to change the direction of his spiritual energy. For this, the Christian religion has received high honor in western culture.

However there are things about Christianity that do not deserve high honors. First and foremost, Christian dogmas have undermined the basis of Christian commitment to spirituality. No dogmas can produce the deepened consciousness that is the substance of the soul. No one can tell a person to violate his intellectual conscience and expect that it will lead to spiritual development. The apotheosis of Jesus and the sanctification of Christian leaders have in no way been helpful to many individuals wishing to develop their own souls. The intelligent individual cannot take his own spiritual consciousness seriously—difficult enough in a materialistic society—when he is confronted with a God descended to earth in human form, with his spirit dwelling in an authoritarian church or a book that is the sole repository of his divine word. These are manifestations of idolatry, which has never led to anything of value in the annals of human spiritual development. Idolatry leads to diminution of the individual and magnification of the idolater. It makes no difference if the idols are golden calves, images of holy men or books cast as sacred writings. An idol means that there is an inappropriate disproportion between what is worshipped and the human worshipper. The center of attention in the human drama is the individual soul struggling to be born; once the center of attention is transferred without, the effort fails, the movement is outward and ultimately materialism prevails.

The production of writings signifying the soul is just that, a signification. The Gospels are what is left to us of the soul of Jesus of Nazareth who gave of himself two thousand years ago to his Jewish countrymen in an obscure corner of the Mediterranean world. They represent an historical event in building souls rather than acquiring power, erecting idols or obtaining wealth. The idolization of Jesus makes superficial his impact on individuals and detracts from their progress in spiritual development. There is no more important idea attributed to Socrates than his self-characterization as midwife, someone who facilitates the development of the mind. In this way, he shielded himself from idolization. There was never a religion of Socrates in the antique world. But Jesus of Nazareth fell victim to the impetus to idolatry that has always been a temptation in human affairs; so much so that Christology has virtually replaced its own message of spiritual consciousness.

It is what emanates from the soul of another human being that is of value in spiritual development. Idolatry is useful for political systems, not for human souls. The impersonal abstractions of Hegel were recognized by Kierkegaard to be of no value to the individual in his confrontation with reality. In truth, the works of Hegel along with most of the systematizing philosophers who followed him have had little to offer humanity except to provide employment for university professors of philosophy. Whatever is of value in philosophy involves one soul communicating with the consciousness of another's with all its feelings and thoughts in full view. Thus even the Gospels are of no value to the individual *kata syneidēsin*—in the sense of higher consciousness—when regarded as a sacred scripture existing on a pedestal. The cosmic spiritual energy can be allowed no favorites and every human being has an equal opportunity to utilize it as he may be able.

Organized Christianity won out over several possible alternatives for the position as the established religion of the Roman Empire; a position that gave it an enormous advantage in the competition of cults that occurred in late antiquity. As spiritual institutions, the competitors appear in any case to have been inferior to Christianity. Some of these were the Egyptian nature cults of Isis and Osiris,

Gnosticism or antique mysticism and the philosophical schools based in Athens, which had grown to resemble the modern world of university philosophy. Against all these movements, Christianity presented the human soul as the central feature of the human condition. However that it was a cult like other cults is undeniable since it was founded upon the apotheosis of a Galilean Jew named Jesus. Once God is believed to have appeared in the image of Jesus Christ, it is but a short step to imagining him speaking through Jesus' disciples, his biographers, his apostles, and through any person who is canonized by an established church. This is the stuff of idolatry and therefore Christianity is not a way of life (as Kierkegaard desperately tried to maintain) but is a cult given to worshipping the symbols of a deity. This fact ought to be faced by those concerned with their souls because the influence of Christianity in present day society stands in the way of spiritual development. One day it must be retired so that a more genuine spiritual culture can be evolved within which individuals can develop their interior selves; something that cannot be done by cult worship.

When the apostle Paul visited Athens, it is recorded that he noted an altar with the inscription TO AN UNKNOWN GOD (Acts 17: 23). Paul regarded this as evidence of the misplaced religiosity of the Athenians and used it as an opportunity to preach the Christian gospel. But the altar to an unknown God was really an example of the negative theology of Athenians. There are no doctrines or commandments associated with an unknown God; he is a symbol that there is more to heaven and earth than men's philosophies or religions. Paul lectured to the Athenians about the uselessness of temples made with human hands; one wonders what he would have said about the cathedrals and churches of today. The modest altar of the Athenians was only a reminder that there were limits to the scope of human perceptions. The concept of an unknown God facilitates consciousness of these limits and thereby opens the door to consciousness of the interior self. More than that, theology cannot do.

The religious tyrannies, cruelties and wars in western societies have given place to a kind of mutual agreement that the religious beliefs of everyone should be respected. Religious criticism occurs only within the confines of religious institutions among their adherents who may differ on points of doctrine. Tolerance is the credo of the times. In Christianity, there is a general movement toward eclecticism, even to the point of envisioning some day a gradual reunification of all the sects. The significant decision for an individual today is to decide whether he is religiously minded, not his thinking about any particular point of religious doctrine. If he is, he may then turn to a sect according to his taste, much like he would choose a neighborhood to live in or a school for his children. Religiosity in the United States means turning to one of the established religious institutions just as an interest in politics means turning to one of the established political parties. (This is less true with

Roman Catholicism where persons tend to maintain loyalty to the ancestral religion.)

However, religious consciousness *kata syneidēsin* is not a matter of religious affiliation or loyalty, it is a matter of an individual seeking to strengthen his soul. The Unknown God whom he may acknowledge has no interest in religious affiliations. Schopenhauer asserted that religion is the "metaphysics of the people," because the "people" are incapable of interior development without the supportive structure of a religious institution. In an age of literacy and education, however, it is high time that people discard the training wheels of religious institutions and recognize the experience of inwardness by which, on his own, the individual develops his consciousness of a personal incorporeal reality called the soul. Historical Christianity provided a model for this inwardness but its institutions have long since themselves become the principal features of the religion. Like a once great leader that has become senile, Christianity is now the main spiritual problem of western society. It is high time that the soul as deepened consciousness be disconnected from Christology. It is high time for Christianity to be placed among the revered institutional ancestors of western culture, alongside Stoicism, Epicureanism, Neoplatonism and Aristotelianism—doctrines that are worthy of scholarly study but which no longer provide an adequate framework upon which to base interior development.

7. Creativity: Voice of the Soul

LIKE MOST HUMAN ACTIVITIES, the arts serve a number of purposes in human affairs. It is essential to be clear about these purposes in order to make sense of the often convoluted relationship of the soul to art. *Kata syneidēsin,* art is the objectification of consciousness; this urge to give objective form to awareness seems to be a kind of instinct accompanying deepening of consciousness. Of course, people are involved with the arts in other ways—entertainment, beautification, investment and livelihood to name a few. However, this discussion is confined to art as an *expression of the soul* of the artist. By art, is meant all forms of creative expression; literature, philosophy, the visual arts, and, what is not usually thought of as art, religious thought.

When an individual reaches a certain level of awareness of the nature of reality surrounding him and of his own interior self, there arises the desire for expression of this awareness. The form embodying this expression is determined by the background, education and temperament of the individual. This urge toward self-expression is seen in primitive art and in children before they are exposed to the constraints of societal conventions. Only certain individuals progress on into mature artistic expression.

What does it mean when a mature individual spontaneously develops his ability to express himself in a creative art form? There is no evident biological value in such activity—there are usually no concrete benefits to be expected from undertaking creative art. There are few individuals who do not know that financial remuneration for artists, whether visual, musical or literary, is a most uncertain affair. Private enterprise or salaried work is far more reliable means of making money. What creative expression seems to represent is a breaking out of the interior self through the shell of physical existence; an event revealing the presence of an interior consciousness that never could be divined from normal surface activities. In creative expression, the soul enters into the material world; it is thrown out into the familiar time-space continuum of biological life for no reasons other than those stemming from its own dynamic.

This form of expression may involve the highest possible level of consciousness. Max Stirner said that he composed philosophical writings for the same reason that birds sing their song in the trees; it represented some fundamental aspect of his nature. Nikolai Berdyaev, the greatest twentieth century philosopher of the spirit, said that he wrote his works out of a visceral need that could only be satisfied at his writing desk. Many writers, painters, sculptors and musicians have expressed similar sentiments, all converging on the awareness that within them there is an urge to expression, which is all but irresistible. An interior energy exists that must be transformed into objective form. In this transformation, the soul comes to terms with its existence in the realm of materiality and emerges as a metaphysical entity. The physical self is subordinated to the soul. And one should include religious expression in this depiction of the creative impulse.

Thus any creative expression *kata syneidēsin,* must embody a consciousness existing within the soul of the artist, otherwise it is not art as so defined. Creative expressions of an individual represent artifacts of great value; like fossil fuels within the earth, they contain stores of spiritual energy of incalculable benefit to mankind. Unlike fossil fuels, however, their energy is not dissipated but is increased with use. One may call the recognition and dissemination of this energy within society by the name *culture,* acknowledging, however, like the name *art,* a great many lesser processes may be included under these categories.

It is evident that the quality of art so defined is dependent on the substance of the consciousness and the faithfulness with which it is represented. One may imagine that some cosmic plan has so ordered the human condition that an incorporeal soul can only communicate with other souls through the material world. Art forms allow souls to experience each other. One does not experience the soul of another through appearance, behavior or transmission of information. At most, one can only surmise personality traits through these features. One learns about other souls through expression in art. The purity of art freed from external pressures determines the spiritual purity of a society. Although this is an ideal to be approached rather than achieved, it is only through this ideal that the individual can surmount what Wassily Kandinsky, the great advocate of the spiritual in art, called "the nightmare of materialism" that turns human life into "an evil useless game."

However...as in all human affairs, there are other sides to art. There are psychological and economic aspects of the human condition that intrude into all human activities. The creation of art in all its forms has been professionalized and institutionalized, and artists desire recognition and compensation for their work. This need for recognition and compensation takes the creative impulse out of the domain of spiritual expression and subjects it to societal influences that have to do with other things than the soul. The focus passes from the interior self to the exterior world, from the individual to society. The distinction between artwork as a pleasure vehicle for an audience and artwork as objectification of the soul all too easily becomes blurred.

Here one enters an area in which it is necessary to be absolutely clear-minded. There is no person who has ever lived on this earth who has not needed the support of his society to some degree. A person cannot live without food and water, without clothing and shelter, without the essential supports that civilization provides according to geographical and social situations. The development of agriculture, sanitation, public services and civic standards has been essential for the human race. No individual can survive without access to the benefits of his society. These facts of life cannot be denied by anyone who pledges allegiance to reality. The advice of Diogenes and Jesus was not good in this area; human beings are not protected by nature and cannot live like packs of dogs or lilies in the field (even the son of God is said to have complained about his accommodations!). There is the requirement of security before individuals can make anything of their souls; otherwise, they fall victim to the assaults of unfeeling, impersonal nature. Those who imagine differently are merely relying upon the civilized capital amassed by others.

Expressing the soul, however, is an issue entirely separate from the requirements of civic life. It has to do with the metaphysical domain of the interior self since souls are not part of a material world; they are part of a spiritual world that has nothing to do with sanitation, food supply or civic standards. For this spiritual world to thrive, it is necessary for the individual to be conscious of its existence and value it beyond the material world even if, at the same time, it is dependent upon the latter for coming into being. The awareness of the *plurality of the dimensions of being* is required for human life to fulfill itself—materiality, life and soul are three of these dimensions but there is nothing sacred about a trinity, perhaps this is an oversimplification and human existence is more complex.

Without openness toward the plurality of being, one is forever chained to the surface consciousness of the material world. The monism of science may facilitate human survival and dominance of nature but it is incompatible with a deepened consciousness. To introduce the materialist worldview into spiritual expression is to transform its essential quality of spirituality. Materialist societies never pay anyone to express their souls; they pay for pleasure, diversion, instruction, acquisition—anything that will relieve the monotony of materialist life. The creative spirit who has not arrived at this realization will never comprehend his relationship to society.

An individual who has not come to terms with the economic and social circumstances of his existence and yet expects to spiritually develop himself is like a child who has not yet learned to walk attempting to ascend a mountain. It is an unreal expectation; it leads to constant deceit—deceit of self and deceit of others. The lack of separation of the material goals of life from the spiritual ones is what results in the hidden psychological and monetary agendas that are so often present in purportedly high-minded activities. The expressive individual who is basically attuned to the needs and desires of his societies may perform socially desirable functions but is not, as Kandinsky put it in his little book

Concerning The Spiritual in Art, "attuned to the inner need that springs from the soul."

To those who do not recognize the soul as a distinct feature of the human condition, these remarks may appear to be without any meaning and certainly without relevance to contemporary life. Most artists and writers fervently wish to be rewarded by society and live with this dream. The fantasies of enthusiastic audiences, impressed critics, wealthy purchasers, widespread readerships are not far from the mind of most contemporary creative individuals. They are so conditioned by society. They usually imagine themselves to be professional artists, writers or philosophers rather than individuals with souls who create artwork. In the current age, in which the "nightmare of materialism" is an ever present reality, the existence of the soul is a nebulous idea, even in the minds of creative individuals for whom it should be the most real of subjects.

Genuine art, literature and philosophy spring from the voice of the soul; the refinements of technique applied to this voice is a subordinate step—the spirit adapting itself to contemporary standards. It hardly needs saying that technique is necessary; one must learn to write before creating literature. But it is generally overemphasized. A materialistic society is always more responsive to technique than to spiritual content; the individual committed to art as the expression of the soul must not allow himself to be seduced by siren songs about technique. The soul must have its say. It is as simple as that.

The labels of artist, writer or thinker are just more roles that societies are so adept in putting on the individual. There is nothing wrong in filling a role of artist just as one might fill roles as doctor, lawyer, plumber or trash collector. But every individual needs to develop his or her soul and this requires its expression. The individual who is not clear about his individuality as distinct from professionalism, who does not distinguish between serving his soul and serving society, who deludes himself into thinking that the needs of his soul and the interests of society are identical, is headed for ignominious failure as a spiritual person. It is then much easier to ignore self-expression entirely and limit one's existence to societal service than to think that creative activity can somehow be performed both for the inner self and the outer world.

Professionalization of the creative impulse causes material motives to intrude upon its expression *kata syneidēsin*. A creative person of any type in our society is required to obtain a great deal of training and experience to achieve the technical skills necessary for his work to be taken seriously. Most people regard the creation of art as a task to be accomplished only by highly trained people who have devoted years to the acquisition of their skills. Writing, music, painting, plastic arts—all these are thought to require a great deal of training for the execution of effective expression. Most people who are interested in art view themselves as connoisseurs who think to enrich their lives by virtue of exposure to art forms. Connoisseurship, not amateurism, is the ideal of the cultured person who aspires to elevate his life. This is the 'grand illusion' of culture since development of the soul occurs not by connoisseurship but by creative activity.

The professional artist, meanwhile, has devoted so much energy to his artwork that he has little left over to acquire a remunerative occupation and must of necessity look to his art to provide a living for himself, not to speak of a dependent spouse and children. (In former times, a mistress was included among the dependents but today this is less common.) The possibility of providing for his material needs through his art seems eminently desirable. The dedicated artist usually feels he has put more than enough time and energy into his work to justify remuneration, and if he strikes it rich, he thinks he is more deserving than a lottery winner who has hit the jackpot. Financial remuneration allows him to produce more artwork, which further strengthens the bonds between himself and admiring audiences. Such is the conventional wisdom about creative persons, artwork and financial remuneration.

The attitude outlined above is perfectly understandable and quite reasonable as an approach toward the role of art and artist in society—as long as one ignores the question of the soul. If the soul is a concept based upon an outdated, pre-scientific view of human beings, then everything is quite reasonable. However, if a human individual's principal task in his life is to create his soul, and if this involves the type of self-expression that strengthens the soul and if the only way that this can occur is through unhindered creative activity—then the conventional wisdom is dangerous since it leads individuals down paths that will be no more fulfilling for their spiritual needs than is the professional activity of a lawyer or plumber. If the creation of the soul is the overriding necessity of human life, then the one thing needful is to redirect one's energies from societal expectations to the needs of the interior self.

It is not enough merely to be able to survive, procreate and amuse oneself. A human being requires more in order to justify the inordinate difficulties of life. In the search for a soul, one cannot have divided purposes; it is necessary to be single-minded in the effort of interior development if the search is not to be aborted prematurely. The soul must have its opportunity to speak freely or else it will never emerge from the darkness of non-expressiveness.

Expression of a deepened consciousness cannot be delegated to others, any more than speech can be delegated to others. A ghostwriter belongs in politics, not in development of the individual. The latter cannot abdicate his soul's expression to professionals no matter how much they appear to be 'under authority' and have the answers to the problems of expression. Everywhere there are culture and religion mongers with hidden agendas who parasitize on naïve individuals seeking to develop themselves. A totally new view of personal development is needed in a society suffering from the twin evils of religious authoritarianism and dogmatic scientism. The creation of art is not some kind of harmless hobby, it is the voice of the soul being heard in a material universe. It is not a profession, anymore than being intelligent, self-reliant or compassionate can be a profession. Every individual in the course of his life needs to develop intelligence, self-reliance and compassion. It is also necessary to express his interior self through creative expression and thereby give greater scope to his soul.

8. Personal Intuitions and Metaphysical Beliefs

AWARENESS OF ONE'S SOUL is an intuition that is immediately available to every thinking person regardless of his education or ideology. *Cogito ergo sum*, I think therefore I am, does not require any special training other than a reflective consciousness. No higher education or mystical experience is necessary for an individual to *intuit* that the core of his being is not his physical organs but his conscious feeling mind. The spiritually developed mind is distinguished linguistically from utilitarian mental activity in most cultures; it is only in societies in which materialism has been invested with the qualities of religious belief that educated individuals resist the idea of the soul.

In the past, awareness of interior being (soul) has been what distinguished advanced societies from primitive ones whose metaphysical impulses were projected into nature or royal gods. The ancient Greeks thought that what distinguished their civilization from barbarian races was individual free will, a concept necessarily requiring an interior self. Jesus' initial ministry was to the Jews, "the people of God," since it was doubtful to him that the *ethnoi* were sufficiently spiritually developed to receive his message. In time, this idea was reversed so that the Christian theologians of Europe regarded Jews as fixed within a materialist worldview.

The notion of free will has always been a corollary of a metaphysical self since it is a fixed property of matter that all its movements are subject to the laws of causality. The stimulus-response view of human behavior is the logical consequence of the absence of belief in a non-material soul. Scientifically-minded materialists who smile at reference to the soul, yet are vociferous in their defense of their rights of traditional American freedoms—including academic freedom, scientific freedom, religious freedom, etc.—have not really thought through their position, or perhaps do not care to. Any freedom referred to human behavior assumes the presence of an independent interior self, free from domination by laws of causality. (Many Christian theologians have insisted that sinfulness of the soul can only be redeemed through divine grace, a kind of spiritual determinism that is analogous to the materialist form.)

The fact is that intuition of one's own soul as a distinct reality invariably emerges in individuals who have reached a certain level of conceptual development. It is the central metaphysical intuition out of which religious ideas appear.

Ideas about an all powerful transcendent God and the immortality of the soul are derivative from primary intuition of one's own soul, and are based on a different type of cognition, that of *metaphysical speculation* rather than *immediate intuition*. The metaphysical beliefs of most people are borrowed from the minds of metaphysically imaginative individuals whose thoughts have become canonical. Such metaphysically imaginative individuals appear throughout history; such must have been Moses and the Hebrew prophets, such were the apostle Paul and the early doctors of the church, especially Origen and Augustine. Others falling into this category are Plotinus, Mohammed, Martin Luther, John Calvin and, more contemporaneously, Joseph Smith, Mary Baker Eddy and Bahaullah.

An individual derives awareness of his own soul from his own existence; however, almost invariably, he derives his ideas about God from the beliefs that his society provides for him. If he is exposed to these beliefs during his formative years, they may become so embedded in his psychological structure that he cannot conceive of them not being grounded in reality. However, they do not derive from his own experience (direct revelations of God are extremely rare and are always suspect); rather they are concepts grafted upon his mind by external authorities. In a society in which there is no tradition of a transcendent almighty deity (e.g. Buddhism), an individual is not likely to come to such beliefs himself. But every individual is conscious of his own soul. This consciousness is an existential fact while thoughts of God, divine judgment and immortality are usually metaphysical beliefs stemming from the imaginative speculations of others.

Immanuel Kant, the first philosopher since Aristotle to bring a genuinely scientific mentality to philosophy, asserted that metaphysics—as distinguished from reason (i.e. science)—had as the proper object of its inquiries three ideas; God, free will and immortality (*Critique of Pure Reason*). In these areas he made his celebrated statement that he had "found it necessary to deny knowledge in order to make room for faith." Kant was basically interested in the forms of cognition rather than the nature of the soul, which as an advocate of the ancient *skepsis*, he doubted could ever be ascertained. The immense influence of Kant further strengthened the already prevalent tendency in philosophy to leave matters of the soul to professional clergy.

If Kant was a pioneer in drawing a distinction between metaphysical belief and rational thought, Kierkegaard made the more important distinction between rational thought and existential awareness. "Truth is subjectivity"—this was Kierkegaard's declaration of independence from the 'rational' world he found to be unreal, hypocritical and unfulfilling. In his *Concluding Unscientific Postscript,* Kierkegaard's magnum opus, he advances the furthest in establishing his own concept of inwardness, i.e. orientation to the soul, as the goal of human development. It all becomes clear (somewhat convolutedly) when Kierkegaard defines faith, "By relating itself to its own self and by willing to be itself, the self is grounded transparently in the Power which constituted it." Kierkegaard knows very little about this Power but a great deal about his self.

Kierkegaard grew up in the home of a religiously fanatical, domineering father who indoctrinated his children with the kind of doctrinaire Christianity that is rarely encountered today. It is surprising that Kierkegaard never seemed to distinguish between his own personal development and the psychological residua of his father's influence. His loyalty to his father—and to his father's concept of Christianity—never wavered. ("A faithful son loves unchangeably.") The same remarkable force of personality he brought to his philosophy, he applied to his paternal relationship. But we, his readers, are entitled to distinguish between his own highly original intuitions and his rigid loyalty to his father and the latter's religiosity.

There was a time when the expression 'soul' was rarely uttered without the modifying adjective 'immortal.' It was natural to think that while the material body decayed into dust, the nonmaterial soul would exist forever. This idea did not arise from any human experience but from the widespread human desire for immortality. It was never possible for intelligent people to believe in the mythic fountain of youth; the decay of the human body has always been seen to be inevitable. The wish to live on forever that affects most individuals at one time or another is focused on the concept of 'soul,' since a metaphysical, indestructible soul has the possibility of living on indefinitely. This desire has been elaborated into complex 'karmic' schemes in Hindu and Buddhist eschatology; as part of the western infatuation with eastern religion, these schemes have been widely disseminated in popular writings. The tendency is most pronounced in theosophy in which the teachings of Madame Blavatsky promised eternal life to the souls of the enlightened ones. Belief in the rebirth of the soul became a self-fulfilling prophecy; lack of belief resulted in dissolution of the soul. The problem of existence is not so compelling when there are many existences to come in the future.

It is to Kierkegaard's credit that he says virtually nothing about immortality or resurrection in all of his writings. He was aware that spiritual existence had to do with "the present moment," not with future moments. With a similar attitude, Thoreau's celebrated deathbed disavowal of interest in a future life was summed up by his answer to a question of what he expected from the next life, "One world at a time." The concept of the soul as an incorporeal reality does not entitle it to be placed in a time frame stretching to infinity. There is nothing to be said about the future state of the soul; there are no temporal attributes to a metaphysical state without material connection. Even to speculate about longevity of the soul fosters the misconception that it is some kind of cerebral offshoot. There is a connection between brain and soul, but what that is has always been and doubtless will always be a great mystery. The soul occupies a different dimension of being than does the physical body and it is best to leave it at that.

To the extent that souls require physical substrates to communicate with the world, one may say that physical and historical circumstances affect the soul. To the extent that the life of the body and the state of the soul seem to share a common energy, one may conclude that they are interrelated. However, when life ends in a human body, when its physical mechanisms cease functioning, it is meaningless to talk of survival of the soul, just as meaningless as it would be to talk of survival of life without a bodily substrate. There is no spiritual experience apart from the living physical self; there is only fantasy founded upon wishfulness. Such fantasies are unrelated to reality and serve only to provide false palliation for the dread of death that every human being must overcome. Heraclitus, the most profound source in ancient Greek philosophy, informed the world that what awaits them after death they can neither expect nor imagine. Individuals have more than enough to do to create conditions in which the soul flourishes during their lifetime; it is empty verbiage to dwell on hopes of another.

The imagination is a most unusual quality of the human mind. Through imagination, the individual asserts his independence of reality. Children love to be exposed to the imaginative arts because it frees them from the oppressive restraints of the world that is. Poetic imagination is the wonderful tool permitting the soul to soar freed from the harsh realities of life. However when imagination is confused with intuition, when the products of imagination begin to be thought of as having a real existence in the world, then imagination is corrupted and becomes an evil affecting society. This corruption in the sphere of religion is called gnosticism, the tendency to believe the products of religious imagination have an independent existence outside of the mind of the imaginer. It can be seen in its fullest flower in the Apostle's Creed, not one word of which is based on a direct experience of the soul, at least not any souls currently extant. Of all the gnosticisms enumerated by the saintly Bishop Irenaeus in his diatribe against heresies, none were so bold as the accepted tenets of organized Christianity. When Irenaeus unblushingly accused the other gnostics of "ascribing to the Divine Word the things that happen to human beings and that they themselves experience," he is laying bare the nature of Christian doctrines. When a person says out of the fullness of his own experience, "If I do not have love, I have nothing," his soul is speaking, but when the ecclesiast solemnly pronounces from his pulpit, "God is love," it is gnosticism.

The problem with gnosticism is that it endows the products of the religious imagination with real existence, from which it is only a short step to canonizing it. What someone says under canonical authority does not stem from the soul but from authority and what is said derives its validity not from the interior self of the speaker but from the authority under which he speaks. The centurion who said to Jesus "I too am a man under authority," he knew exactly from whence his authority derived, the power of Rome. Authority exists in governments, armies, corporations and many other types of organizations dedicated to material life. However, there is no such thing as authority in matters of religion because the soul does not participate in organizational activities. Martin Luther claimed this freedom from authority in matters of religion for himself—if unfortunately not for others. There is no place for obedience in matters of religion *kata syneidēsin*, there is only the virtue of intellectual conscience.

The soul's existence has nothing to with the following representations made by religious institutions: 1) knowledge about an almighty God who is the maker of the universe and who requires of humans certain beliefs and behaviors; 2) knowledge of a human being who had a unique relationship with God; 3) claim that a certain elect people have a special relationship with God; 4) preaching of an afterlife involving damnation of sinners and rewards for the faithful; 5) assertion that their institution provides authority in spiritual matters and miracles. The soul knows none of these things except as dogmas imposed by organizations whose leaders are subject to all the human failings of self-interest, pride, love of power and fear of change. Gnostic teachings are very convenient to institutions and serve to keep the 'children of faith' within traditional confines. Reliance on the force of tradition to sustain religious dogmas is a great error as Clement of Alexandria, the philosophically learned catechist of early Christianity, pointed out when his religion was still young and striving to displace the popular religions of his times.

A soul comes to consciousness through experience and expression; without its *own* experience and its *own* expression, it can know nothing and lives the sleeplike state described by the antique philosophers. There are no authorities for the soul; there is only the experience of other souls derived from life and art. The most iniquitous aspect of spiritual authority is that it stands in the way of spiritual fulfillment of individuals through propaganda claiming possession of spiritual gnosis. Scribes and Pharisees seem to abound throughout human history. But every individual starts afresh in life with a spiritual potential and is placed under no authority for the solution of spiritual problems. There are no Holy Churches, Holy Scriptures or Revealed Creeds that can serve as an *authority* for the nascent spiritual consciousness. They can only provide insights into the minds of other individuals. Every person must strike out on his or her own in the adventure of spiritual existence.

The crucial fact of western societies is not that they have lost the capacity for faith, it is that they have lost trust in the gnosticisms of their churches. The psychological forces acting to strengthen the churches—inertia connected with the existent, pleasures derived from maintaining traditions, fear of fundamental change—all these have not been sufficient to keep Gnostic teachings alive in the minds of intelligent individuals. The fateful division of believers into clergy and laity, into those with special access to Gnostic mysteries and those without this access, has been disastrous for spiritual fulfillment. Simplified creeds are no longer sufficient, individuals with developed minds want vital spiritual experiences—if they do not obtain them from their religions, they look elsewhere. The whole bursting out of the peoples of Europe into the world at large with all its consequences for the other peoples of the earth may have stemmed in part from the loss of trust in Gnostic dogmas regulating their lives.

Individuals in their mental prime have not merely lost interest in beliefs such as God, immortality and judgment day, they have also lost interest in the concept of the soul as a spiritual reality. Soul consciousness has become enmeshed in the general crisis of disinterest in religion engulfing religions; the individual who gives only a superficial allegiance to the teachings of his religion gives only a surface allegiance to the idea of the soul, which is an integral part of that teaching. Religious fundamentalism is merely a temporary solution as no form of belief that defies the intellectual conscience of mankind can long play an important role in society. *Materialism is not the cause of the decline of religions; it is its consequence.* When persons no longer believed in the idea of God, some psychological quirk induced them to cast their whole consciousness of the soul and its affairs into the trashcans of *Geistesgeschichte.*

Heinrich Heine who said that God was dying and Friedrich Nietzsche who thought Him dead (diagnosing His terminal illness as grief over the human race—*Also Sprach Zarathustra*) did not notice that it was not only God who was failing, but the human soul along with Him. Rebuilding the consciousness of soul is the task of an enlightened society. In order to realize his or her own soul, it is essential for the individual to have consciousness of it as the highest and most important reality of the human condition.

9. The Materialist Ideology

THE PROBLEM OF THINKING about the soul involves one's orientation to reality. The expression 'soul' is used today as a poetical figure of speech, a literary metaphor, perhaps also as part of traditional religious discourse, but not as a reality-based term. The scientific enlightenment of the past two centuries has resulted in discarding beliefs that have no basis in reality. Liberation from superstitions of every type, including religious superstitions, has permitted 'enlightened' individuals to discard notions that involve one with only words instead of facts. Jean-Paul Sartre, in his remarkable mental autobiography *Les Mots*, commented that it took him thirty years to get over the "philosophical idealism" that was the heritage of his French-Christian upbringing. Sartre's famous phrase "Existence precedes essence" was the statement of a realist disabused of the patriotic and religious humbug of his childhood. Sartre's ideals were that of a contemporary realist (not the medieval form), that is to say his ultimate ideal was the material universe, the concrete reality of the here and now. Flesh and blood, not the soul, was the human ideal of Sartre; one that he shared with most of the bourgeois world regardless of political ideology. Insofar as he idolized the concrete and feared illusion, he was in the camp of the bourgeoisie, albeit of the intellectual leftwing variety (deceptively calling his activities 'intersubjectivity').

However, in spite of Sartre's acknowledged intellectual powers, the notion that the materialist mentality is founded upon a more honest insight into reality does not stand up to intellectual analysis. The materialist ideology (not materialistic values, which are something different although related) assumes that only what is presented to the senses is real. As creatures of our senses, we can only know about existence that comes to us through them. Our mind may be wonderfully facile, but reality is what is presented to it through the media of the five senses. Thus, insofar as one is interested in the world of reality, he must be dependent on his senses for the basic information. Such is the view of the materialist if he is provoked into explicating what seems to him to be an obvious truism. The materialist worldview has a long philosophic history beginning with John Locke and extending through Karl Marx albeit this is rarely invoked by materialist-minded people of today.

The obvious truism of materialism, as Kant pointed out a long time ago, turns out to be false. The fact is that the senses provide us with a very defective image of the real world, at least the real world discovered by scientists with their superior means of studying material objects. The structure of the universe appears to have only the faintest relationship to the images presented by the human sensory apparatus. What we see and hear during a thunderstorm bears no similarity to the nature of lightning and thunder disclosed by physicists. One could multiply examples endlessly, discussing every aspect of the perceptible world, in which the evidence of science shows that our senses provide an unreal image of the world around us.

Nevertheless, these kinds of thoughts that are certainly not new have had no effect on the materialist ideology that it alone has insight into the real world. This is because this view is not truly based upon *knowledge* of reality, it is based upon *control* of reality. This is what attracts materialists of every stripe. It provides techniques for dominating the outer world; mere consciousness of reality really has very little to do with the materialist worldview. Its power explains why aborigines of primitive lands convert en masse to European Christianity or Arab Islam, and that the culture of the United States of America is rapidly spreading through the civilized—and not so civilized—world. Power attracts the human psyche, it is intoxicating to men and, as a noted statesman recently remarked, it is aphrodisiac to women. Technology, which is the principal offshoot of materialism, has allowed humans to control the whole world of nature, including other humans. When, materialistically-speaking, one talks of the "real world," one is not referring to a philosophical concept, one is talking about property, power and control. Fundamentally, the materialist ideology is the culmination of the biological instincts of survival and propagation, and, as Freud postulated, most human behaviors, civilized, erotic or otherwise, have to do with these instincts. Materialistic values regard the mind as merely a useful tool for gratification of instinctual desires. In developed materialist societies, property and power represent survival and propagation but their biological origin is unmistakable.

Assuredly, therefore, the control over nature deriving from a materialist mentality does not provide for a deeper consciousness of reality. One may be quite effective in clearing a wilderness of all plant and animal life, but this is not a testimonial to one's knowledge of nature. There is a growing awareness in the world that control of nature may not be the be-all and end-all of civilization; it may be that something more is needed to fulfill human needs. It is not likely that this something more will be an expansion of the materialist ideology. External orientation inevitably leads to forms of domination; whereas an internal orientation leads to consciousness of inner reality. The reality disclosed by looking to the internal self is more valid and more intense than that provided by the materialist worldview because nothing is more surely existent than our consciousness of self, our soul. The entire calling into question of the evidence of the senses by modern science has not shaken the validity of *cogito ergo sum*.

It is necessary to admit philosophers have often fallen victim to the seductions of the scientific-materialistic world-view. Descartes himself justified his philosophical quest through the promise of control of nature (*Discourse de la Méthode*). It was not enough for him that he should explore his own soul as the Greek philosophers had, he went on to promise that his 'method' would make men *maîtres et possesseurs de la Nature*. Although Descartes subjected himself to considerable ridicule by proposing a number of erroneous scientific theories (notably localization of consciousness in the pineal gland), his intuition was correct; one could control nature through dispassionately conducted scientific activity. Here was the European materialist mentality emerging in the heart of philosophical epistemology. In time, Descartes' interest in knowledge for its own sake became a side issue, control of the material world was all that really counted. Today, when gigantic mega-scientific and mega-engineering activities expend billions of dollars in countless technological projects and philosophy is only one of the lesser handmaidens of society, domination of the external world is the single significant issue. Cartesianism has become a monster in the hands of modern science.

The desires associated with the materialist ideology are familiar ones. Success and failure in the outer world are known entities; one knows what to expect of them. There are the familiar yearnings for money, recognition and power that are the outcomes of material success. The greatest complaint emanating from the poor is not hardship but lack of access to the material good things in life. Preoccupation with recognition and power destroys the motivation to turn inward since they represent the very opposite of inwardness; they represent an excessively high valuation of the outside world. The person who strives for outer directed success cannot strive to develop his interior self since the two values are incommensurable. It is no accident that Jesus, who was the most inwardly directed person depicted in western culture, was also portrayed as the one with least power regarding his own material circumstances. Yet it must be admitted by the most materialistic of individuals that he was a human being who fulfilled his own potential.

The two commandments of a materia-oriented society are to acquire and secure. Thus to the extent that an individual is materially successful in society, security becomes his guiding light, while whose who feel themselves unsuccessful are absorbed with acquisition. This situation has been described with incomparable clarity by R.H. Tawney in his 1920 classic, *The Acquisitive Society*. The basic characteristic of the members of this society is that "their whole tendency and interest and preoccupation is to promote the acquisition of wealth." Tawney believed that the entire modern world had fallen under the spell of this conception. His observations are truer today than they were in 1920. Not only are the industrialized nations of the world preoccupied in this manner, but all the 'undeveloped' areas have become similarly entranced. Tawney believed that somehow modern societies needed to subordinate individual economic ends for the good of society as a whole. One is entitled to be skeptical of approaches founded upon Utopian socialist ideas. But Tawney perceived better than most that if "men do not possess their own souls," they will possess the earth and destroy the face of nature. Like most twentieth century scientifically-minded individuals, Tawney (an economist by training) used the term 'soul' as a literary device; he might not have wanted to be pinned down on the meaning of the word. He certainly did not elaborate on how one possesses his own soul.

It is beyond human ability for individuals to fully participate in the acquisitive society and yet possess their own souls. God-fearing Christian that he was, Tawney thought that what a man is worth is "a matter between his own soul and God." But if men and women have only an incipient soul to begin with and must utilize their energies to realize this soul, it is not enough to leave the matter to God. It is not enough to merely avoid preoccupation with acquisition; one must have a preoccupation with the realization of his soul. This preoccupation demands as much time, energy and thought as the preoccupations of the materialist worldview. The materialist view of reality invariably diverts one from formation of his soul.

10. Philosophy and Philosophers

EVERY THOUGHTFUL PERSON HAS a 'philosophy.' He may not recognize it as such, it may not be at the forefront of his consciousness, he may regard it as common sense adjustment to the realities of the world. But genuine philosophy means more than common sense, it means reflection on the nature of reality beyond what is presented to the senses, and the orientation of the self to this reality. Thus philosophy at some level must involve metaphysics. It is an essential form of thought without which individuals cannot emerge from animal existence. Religiously minded persons have a strong philosophy replete with metaphysical concepts and related value systems. No one can live without any philosophy; if he does not develop one for himself, society will surely provide it for him.

Nevertheless, certain individuals in history have been called philosophers, implying there is something distinctive about their philosophy that separates them from the rest of the population.

Throughout the antique era of philosophy, philosophers were regarded as individuals who *lived* in a certain way. There can be no dispute that there was something unique about the philosophers of the antique Greek world that distinguished them from their compatriots. They were called philosophers because they professed to love wisdom, i.e. philosophy as defined above. Their philosophic beliefs may not have been much different from other educated Greeks, it was only that they were more intensely involved with these beliefs. The nature of this involvement was not only through verbal or literary discourse; they lived according to their philosophy. Their ideas about reality were more important to them than were the prevailing societal values and their lives reflected this valuation. Modern professors of philosophy who do not share this commitment tend not to recognize someone like Diogenes of Sinope as a philosopher because he did not systematically present his ideas; the ancient Greeks, however, regarded him as one of their greatest philosophers because he lived so completely in accord with his concept of reality.

Plato exemplifies the modern concept of the philosopher; namely someone who engages in well-polished literary exposition of his ideas. From the beginning, Plato was clearly different from the traditional type of Greek philosopher because his rhetoric outshone the reputation of his philosophical character. He was a litterateur, a lecturer, an administrator of the Academy but not a stalwart individualist such as Socrates, Antisthenes or Diogenes. To this day, his personality remains nebulous. One view of him by a near contemporary (Timon) runs as follows:

> a sweet-voiced speaker, musical in prose as the cicala who, perched on the trees of Hecademus [the Academy], pours forth a strain as delicate as the lily.
> -- Diogenes Laertius

This had not been the kind of personality attributed to their philosophers by the ancient Greeks.

While one must recognize Plato's contributions to philosophy through his dramatic portrayals of Socrates and his disciples, and his literary sensibilities applied to cosmology, basically Plato appears to have been more of a litterateur than a philosopher of the antique type. Later, because his imaginative visions harmonized with the Christian picture of the universe, he was accorded a place in history far above other pagan philosophers. In modern times, he has been virtually apotheosized by professors of philosophy of all persuasions, even those who themselves have little to do with Plato's brand of philosophical idealism. The alliance of professors and priests regarding Plato has given him a position that is unmatched in the annals of philosophy.

But for an individual seeking direction from philosophy for his own life and his own soul, Plato has little more significance than that of a gifted docudramatist. It is incontrovertible that he made personalities and ideas of ancient Athens come alive in some of his dialogues (some are pure tedium). He was a person who knew how to handle philosophical prose, he was a master of literary characterization and a disciplined writer. We may also imagine he was an effective administrator, establishing the Academy as an institution that maintained its continuity beyond that of all the other philosophical schools at Athens. However the one thing he did not do was to make Plato the philosopher come alive in his writings. We do not experience the soul of Plato. The fact is that insights into him as an individual that can be obtained from his letters and the comments of his contemporaries do not reveal an outstanding individual, certainly not one that is entitled to the near deification he has received in western culture.

When Christianity became the established religion of the Roman Empire, the position of philosophy radically changed. It was no longer the effort on the part of an individual to live out his deepened consciousness but rather served as the 'handmaiden' of church doctrines by explicating and rationalizing the Gnostic dogmas of the Christian establishment. This was the condition of philosophy for as long as Christianity dominated the intellectual life of western civilization. The burning of heretics cowed western intellectuals; it was only in a few remote areas in Europe that men could express themselves freely on philosophical issues. Giordano Bruno was burned at the stake, Descartes feared to publish his writings and Spinoza's writings were placed on the Catholic Index for expressing ideas that today would be regarded as harmless abstractions. It was not until the Enlightenment in Europe that philosophers felt free to express themselves publically as they had in antiquity. By then, however, it was too late for the classical notion of philosophy as a lived activity. The *magic of science* was in the air and philosophy was confined to the museum atmosphere of the universities. Ambitious young people wanted to get in touch with the juggernauts of science. Philosophers jumped on the bandwagon and, with rare exceptions, have not yet descended, albeit that philosophy is the puniest and least significant of all the disciplines dedicated to the proposition that knowledge is power. Philosophers became entrenched in universities as professors whose principal tasks were not discovering truth and confronting reality but gaining tenure and teaching history of philosophy. The minds of philosophers became professionalized and focused on scholarly studies. All this has been related in full by Schopenhauer in his masterful essay 'Philosophy at the Universities.' Nothing more need be added to his remarks even though they were penned more than a century ago. Contemporary analytic philosophy in American and British universities is about as relevant to the human condition as the study of medieval Swiss dialects or Inca architectural techniques.

Regardless of the decline of independent philosophy, *Homo sapiens* still manifests a yearning for a deeper consciousness of reality and a coming to grips with the world *kata syneidēsin*. The perennial turning to religions, traditional and innovative, and the infatuation with Eastern spirituality is evidence of this yearning. There is no human activity more meaningful than the aspiration toward a profound contact with reality. The Portuguese poet Fernando Pessoa, who has now come into his own as one of the most fertile minds of the twentieth century, wrote in a letter to a compatriot, "I call those works insincere...that do not contain a fundamental metaphysical idea, that is to say through which does not pass, be it only as a wind, a notion of the gravity and mystery of Life."

Philosophy is the metaphysics of soul. Søren Kierkegaard concludes his little book *The Point of View for my Work as an Author* with the statement, "Before God, religiously, when I talk with myself, I call my whole literary activity my own upbringing and development." There is no body of knowledge that constitutes philosophy; it is an orientation toward interior reality. One acquires a body of knowledge in order to become a lawyer or a doctor but one does not become a philosopher in such a manner. Cognitive science is not philosophy, it is scientific psychology and has nothing to do with the soul. One learns philosophy by experiencing the minds of individuals who have lived and understood philosophy; thus discipleship is the mark of the student of philosophy rather than enrollment in a graduate program. This type of learning is more difficult in modern civilization but is not impossible. Books and discussions are valuable when they provide a seeker with experiences of the soul of a genuine philosopher. But one's own effort is always the key ingredient.

The problem of soullessness in contemporary society is directly related to the moribund state of philosophy in contemporary culture. When one realizes that religion, which was the surrogate for philosophy for centuries, has now such a peripheral place in culture, it becomes clear why there are so few human models for the individual who has a bent for philosophy. Henry Thoreau remarked a century and a half ago that he had learned nothing of value from his elders, but at least he was free to develop his interior self as he could. Today what is needed is an extensive *apomanthanein*, the unlearning preached by Antisthenes, not of facts, but of the value systems of the materialist ideology. Until this unlearning is performed, there is no time or energy left over for the development of one's soul.

One learns philosophy through experience, reflection on experience and expression of the reflection. The soul is formed in these activities and comes to life much as muscles and tendons are strengthened through physical activity. One expresses himself with philosophy in order to develop his soul; thus the principal beneficiary of philosophical expression, whether it be through literature, art or a lifestyle, is the individual who is expressing himself. There is no one who benefits more by writing a philosophical work than the writer himself who strengthens himself immensely with such an effort. The personality of

Thoreau was greatly formed through his habit of journalizing. Can one imagine a literarily mute Kierkegaard, Nietzsche or Berdyaev? The antique *Nulla dies sine linea*, which can be found at the end of Sartre's *Les Mots*, may be freely translated as "Let not a day pass without attending to your creative self."

Delving into writing by an unfamiliar philosopher is like reading the announcement on a dust cover of a book or previewing a film. It is a hint of what may lie within, of what the substance of the author might contain. No philosophical work *kata syneidēsin* can be fully assimilated without apprehending the interior state and exterior circumstances of the writer. The reader who wishes to become intimately involved with a writer must evaluate all that he has written and penetrate deeply into his life, not to learn biographical trivia, but to understand his personality. Books are the means to the end of experiencing a significant person and in themselves only represent stages on the author's life's way. The same can be said to apply to artists and musicians; if one wishes experiences rather than diversions, the necessary energy must be devoted toward that end. What good can come gazing at the canvases of Edvard Munch or listening to the symphonies of Ludwig van Beethoven without knowing their purposes and personalities? The art of life consists to a great extent of developing the capacities necessary to arrive at important cultural experiences.

In the art form known as philosophy—and philosophy *is* an art form—there is rarely any need to concern oneself with the clerks of academia. Perhaps this attitude applies less to the world of Russian philosophy, but it is largely true for the rest of Europe, and especially Anglo-American philosophy. Few scholars write to develop their souls, they write to develop their careers. Philosophy, however, has nothing to do with scholarly expertise. There is nothing wrong with career development, except that one should be clear about its purpose and place in society. The philosopher one wishes to experience is one who expresses his deepest self in his writings; the difference between this type of expression and scholarly activity is like the difference between poetry and an annotated bibliography.

Critical evaluation in a creative literary art like philosophy is a form of spiritual vivisection that should have no place in culturally advanced societies. Paul Gauguin summarized the situation charitably with his comment, "A critic is someone who minds somebody else's business." There is no purpose served except the self-aggrandizement of the critic; nothing is ever gained by critical studies in expressive literature except facilitating the career of the critic. In fact, considerable harm is often done by subjecting immature minds to the mindset of a critical thinker wielding his analytical knife in the realm of the arts.

One has as much right to dissect the artist's work as he has to dissect the artist. A critic is entitled to his opinion as to whether he is positively or negatively affected by a creative work; the nature of his response is obviously as much a reflection of himself as of the work to which he is reacting. What the public needs from 'critics' is to make the presence of high-minded books and artwork known, perhaps with some allusion to their general nature; more than that is mere presumptuousness.

One might modify Schopenhauer's celebrated phrase about religion ("religion is the metaphysics of the people") and say that philosophy is the religion of a high-minded individual. This religion may require denial of "father and mother and wife and children" because it is not an avocational matter, but a commitment to life *kata syneidēsin*. Above all, what is needed is the requirement of Antisthenes: *to periairein, to apomanthein*—the stripping off, the unlearning.

11. The Materialist Worldview in America

WRITING ABOUT ONE'S SOCIETY negatively seems an ungrateful sort of thing to do if it has not treated the writer in an unpleasant manner. When the German-Jewish intellectuals cursed the society that had exiled them, cast them into concentration camps and ultimately murdered them, one could understand their point of view. In America, however, where writers, comparatively speaking, lead a comfortable life in terms of physical wellbeing, there may be difficulty understanding the vituperation lavished on American society. A critical attitude toward society was not permitted in the Soviet Union, where a critical author would be cast into prison as a "social parasite." We in the United States are expected to be appreciative of the freedom accorded the creative individual, especially the independent philosopher who has virtually no restrictions placed upon his literary expression.

Of course, the main reason a philosopher in the United States is free to say what he wants is that nobody particularly cares what he says no matter how explosive his message may be. If he is not diverting, entertaining or usefully instructive, he is simply ignored. Ideas are not explosive commodities in America as they once were in the days of the founding fathers. The Soviet Union was a society recently established upon a revolutionary idea so that its leadership was apprehensive about ideas in general. However, this sensitivity is changing in contemporary Russia and it appears that it is on the way to reaching a condition in which anyone can write freely about ideas. Perhaps in time it will approach the United States where any idea can be put forth with no danger of imprisonment and no possibility of affecting the public at large. It is this disinterest in ideas that largely accounts for the cynical attitude of most serious American writers toward the society they live in – no one cares what they think.

It was different in the first European settlements in America. The coming of the white man to New England was initiated by English Puritans devoted to a religious *idea.* The idea was not religious freedom *in abstracto* but freedom for themselves to live the religious life they believed in, unhampered by the religious establishment of Great Britain. They were the cutting edge of the Protestant spirit that was beginning to wane in their country. As far as can be told, this was their major motivation for braving the hostile wilderness of seventeenth century New England. It was the health of their souls they were after, not free land or precious metals. They have left few significant literary remains but their chronicles reveal that the first settlers of New England had a powerful sense of the priority of spiritual life. They meant to create a certain kind of spiritual society, sacrificed greatly to that end and would not allow others with different views infringe upon their new world. They were a harsh people. The Puritans did not have a concept of an ideological melting pot, but rather defended the exclusiveness of what they considered to be a spiritually higher way of life. We may disagree with the intolerant features of their life style, but its essential importance is that it was based on a spiritual worldview rather than a materialist one.

In the course of the eighteenth century, the practical Benjamin Franklin rather than the ideological Jonathan Edwards came to represent the American ideal. The materialist worldview was becoming the dominant feature of American society. The American Revolution was essentially a movement for better business conditions—the evil genie of every businessman is taxes and taxes are what triggered the commotion in Boston. The nineteenth century in America, with few exceptions, is one long chronicle of territorial expansionism and subduing of the former inhabitants. Business became the business of America, creating the prototype of the acquisitive society. Immigrants from Europe swarmed like bees to honey to a land where not merely highborn lords but everyone could aspire to the acquisitive life. The United States of America was founded upon the ideal of material success, grew up on the ideal of material success and presently stands firm on its belief that the good life is the life of material success. Technology has replaced the Word of God as the guiding principle of human life. It is as if the Puritans never were; they have been consigned along with the Indian tribes and Mexican pueblos to the realm of history. All that remains of them now are the place names that dot the New England countryside.

Today the citizens of the United States have the rights to life, liberty and the pursuit of happiness (read material success). It seems ironic that the right of life has become the affair of religious fanatics who care nothing for souls as long as every blob of human protoplasm is preserved no matter how rudimentary its condition. The less significance given to the state of souls, the more it is given to biological life. Liberty is like food and water, it is a necessity in human life but hardly sufficient as an end in itself. The pursuit of happiness is the dream of everyone but one must have some sense of where to look. There are many who have suspected that 'happiness' is a chimera, nowhere to be found in this life.

The ancient Greeks admired the philosophic mind that announced, "Best of all is to die, but even better yet is never to have been born." One does not have to subscribe to such extreme pessimism to be confident—as one is confident of few things in life—that the materialist worldview is no guide to the happy state, unless one means by happiness the condition of an infant in a sandbox. The founding fathers hopefully meant happiness *kata syneidēsin.* The fixation of

American society with the young indicates that most adult Americans hope that something will happen to the children of the country, especially their own children, that has not yet happened to them. It is difficult to know how anything will come of a society if its expectations are forever being put onto the next generation. What can be expected of children when they are always the hope of the world? — it is a sure sign of a defective society when the highest good is not a mature adult.

Van Wyck Brooks from the perspective of the literary reformer wrote in 1918 about America society:

> For if our old men of thought come to a standstill at middle age, our old men of action as one sees them in offices, in the streets, in public position, everywhere! are not old men at all but old boys. Graybeards of sixty or seventy, mentally and spiritually indistinguishable from their sons and grandsons, existing on a level of reflection and emotion in no way deeper or richer than their own childhood, they seem to have miraculously passed through life without undergoing any of life's maturing influences.
> -- *Letters and Leadership*

Our old men of action seventy years later have not changed at all; our old men of thought, however, seem to have disappeared completely. With such a perspective as a public literary figure, it is not surprising that Brooks suffered a prolonged nervous breakdown from which he emerged as a more tractable litterateur with less demands to make upon his society.

The state of contemporary American society is like a modern cruise ship equipped with all the conveniences and amenities technology can provide except someone forgot to install the compass. Consequently, although the passengers can have a marvelous time on board, they cannot go anywhere. Since *Homo sapiens* is not born to have a marvelous time but is *born to spiritually go somewhere,* his time on board is often a bitter disappointment unless he manages to remain at the mentality of his childhood.

The apprehension in life that one is on a voyage going nowhere is what leads to the feeling of *Angst. Angst* is not the result of a mismanaged childhood, it is the result of a mismanaged interior self. *Angst* is resolved only when the soul is on the wing, when the energies of the individual are dedicated to powering its flight. Material wellbeing may narcotize this feeling for a time, but it is only narcosis as surely as if an individual were suppressing pain through constant morphine administration. The constant acquisition of things is a form of psychic mainlining; sooner or later, however, the drug fails in its purpose and *Angst* returns. One may spend a lifetime with perpetual acquisitions, trying to keep *Angst* at bay, but this is not a life to recommend to others. A life to be proud of is one in which the individual is not dependent on the endless trivialities of daily existence, but rather one in which he lives from—as Antisthenes put it—his internal riches.

Career, family and the bourgeois life style are the three prime factors that, when unchecked, lead an individual toward spiritual stultification—the tragedy of the might have been or never was. It is not that a career has no value, or that family has no meaning or that acquisitions have no purpose; it is that the materialist worldview sees no other *telos* in life, everything else is entertainment or pleasure-seeking, not to be regarded on the same level as wealth or family. Thoreau commented that society sees a chimney sweep as socially desirable as long as he gets paid for cleaning chimneys. Raising children is a biological mandate valued in all societies. But an individual who views developing his soul as the one thing needful?—one has to correct such a person and help him see the self-indulgent nature of his ways. These attitudes are understandable when one has not apprehended the reality of the soul.

The essential concept of life in America at most levels of society is the notion of generating sufficient income to satisfy one's material desires. Whether one is a real estate developer or heart surgeon, it is the ingathering of wealth that is the criterion of success, for it is what is used to satisfy material expectations. The economic structure of the United States—and most other 'developed' nations—is founded on consumerism powering the never-ending search for new ways of creating wealth. During a time when Wall Street is exhibiting one of its periodic crashes and probably soon to be followed by an economic downturn, our President provides the advice that people should continue buying new products, not abstaining for even the shortest time from their addiction to consumerism (this even though it is clear to all that the economic problems of the country are caused by spending out of proportion to productivity).

The belief that the good life is realized through continually accelerating the earning-spending regimen is so much an article of faith in America that few people imagine a fulfilling life can be lived in any other way. Occasionally, a passionate individual will be gripped by an infatuation—with an idea, with another milieu, with nature or even another individual—and the earning-spending will be suspended for a time. But all infatuations wane and society's basic orientation toward material existence resumes its hold over the individual. This is why infatuations are felt to be the province of the young who can more easily withdraw temporarily from the societal way of life.

Materialist societies view those who fail to participate in earning-spending cycles as failures and those so viewed generally feel themselves to be failures. There is no other route to success except through material success—that is to say accumulation of wealth. Monastic retreat is no longer a valid alternative except for a very few individuals who have been able to maintain a strictly religious attitude toward existence. Idealistic pursuits that are uninvolved with wealth accumulation can hold individuals for a time but, sooner or later, the materialist motif of society wins out. The main thread of the pervasive immigrant history in the United States has been a rush to become rich—or at least comfortably affluent—as quickly as possible.

Economically disadvantaged people have only rarely opted out of the materialist lifestyle; most would like to emulate it and feel themselves to be failures when they fail to do so. Like the adoption of Christianity by black slaves, the underprivileged ethnic and racial groups in the United States want to adopt the materialist ethos of affluent America, but it was easier for black slaves to become Christian than it is today for disadvantaged individuals to become well-to-do bourgeois.

People as members of natural groupings are always materialists since nature knows only improving the material conditions of life. It is the individual who must search out alternative modes of being. The more the society of an individual is oriented toward materiality, the more he has to turn toward his own consciousness. This responsibility cannot be delegated elsewhere or postponed to a subsequent generation because the essential nature of individuality is responsibility toward the self. Obtaining a deepened consciousness is the task of an individual if he wants to be more than a clever brute. The prevailing culture of the United States has never fostered a deepened consciousness after waning of the Puritan spirit. The Puritans may have had many faults but they did have an awareness of themselves as something more than clever brutes. Perhaps their notion of the soul should have been less bound up with religious dogma, perhaps they might have developed more of a sense of themselves as independent souls rather than Christian souls. But they did have a consciousness of themselves as spiritual beings that has long since disappeared.

Perhaps we should imagine Hester Prynne of *The Scarlet Letter* instead of Jonathan Edwards as the true Puritan spirit. Alone in the world, scorned by her contemporaries, this creation of Hawthorne's imaginative genius developed her soul against all odds. Like Cervantes's Don Quixote and Hölderlin's Hyperion, she is that rare fictional character who symbolizes the essential spiritual quality of humanity. We should ask ourselves if existence in the United States today is more conducive to a life *kata syneidēsin* than it was in Puritan New England.

12. A Cosmology for Souls

THE CONCEPT OF THE human condition in antiquity by and large was pitched considerably higher than it is today. Human beings were considered to be at the center of the universe; this was the case in the Ptolemaic cosmology of the heavens or the Biblical cosmogony in which Man represented the final work of God. Present day humans, however, although greatly superior to the people of antiquity with respect to power and knowledge, no longer have a sense of themselves at the center of the universe. The science of astronomy has told them that they are like specks of sand in a limitless cosmos. Whatever powers they may have in their little corner of the world, it remains an exceedingly small corner with respect to the universe as a whole. The Copernican cosmology has produced a radically different self-image for humans. Religions may continue to preach an important relationship between God and man, but the dominant scientific worldview has established the reality of an individual as a virtually imperceptible mite in the enormity of space.

Fundamentalist preachers bring ridicule upon themselves by accepting a biblical model of the universe that is not in accord with instrumental reports to the contrary. The planet earth clearly has no special position in the universe; it is one of many planets in a solar system that is easy to lose among the endless myriads of planetary bodies. The biblical stories of creation, literally interpreted, merely provide amusement to materialist circles, which are sure they know better about the facts of existence. If there is an almighty Creator, it is evident that he had a lot more on his mind than our tiny corner of the universe; it was a miracle, perhaps, that he remembered to populate it at all. From the point of view of astrophysics, metaphysics is merely the imaginative quality of the mind by which people are prone to console themselves. A more persuasive argument than Auschwitz against God the Father is the Milky Way.

There can be no questioning Copernican astronomy on its own terms. It is based on scientific observations of the visible universe that do not admit serious contradiction. From a spiritual perspective, however, an entirely different cosmology can be constructed. The physical universe is to the incorporeal soul as the sum total of carbon atoms on the planet is to a living organism; it is a necessary background phenomenon, but one that exists on a different plane of being. The occurrence of souls on the planet Earth seems to be a unique event. There is no evidence that this phenomenon exists anywhere else in the universe—except in the minds of science fiction writers who make careers out of imagining higher life forms elsewhere. It defies materialist logic to believe that our physically insignificant planet should harbor such a unique form of existence. The contemporary world thinks there must be other forms of life, not to speak of consciousness, out there somewhere in the heavens.

So astronomers continue to constantly improve their telescopes scanning heavenly bodies light years away and scrutinizing photographs from distances incomprehensible to the human mind—but there are no signs of life, intelligent or otherwise. If the results of astronomical investigations were judged by any ordinary criteria, it would have been long concluded that we, *Homo sapiens*, are the only intelligent life and that life on our planet is the only life of any type in the universe. It is mental resistance that compels us to refuse to accept this preeminent position and draw the necessary conclusions. Our society dreams of other forms of life in the universe for the same reason former ages dreamt of God and his cohorts in a heavenly abode. It is resistance to assuming responsibility for one's own significance. The speculations of those imagining the existence of life elsewhere in the universe are about as likely as those of creationists dogmatizing about our origins.

One may imagine, if it is desired to create a cosmology more suitable to the human condition, that primal being is energy, diffused and concentrated in myriad ways in a multidimensional universe. Matter is the form of this energy most familiar to us since our sensory apparatus has developed in order to relate to material existence. Life is a different form of matter; it is inanimate matter transformed to a new level of existence in which the laws of physics are transcended by the laws of biology. And we humans, representing conscious life and possessing souls, manifest a still greater transformation of being; as much a leap from unconscious life as life was from inanimate existence. We are subject to spiritual laws in addition to those of physics and biology that control lower forms of being. Consciousness of self and of other souls is the center of a spiritual cosmology of a higher order of reality than the Copernican one. If this is mystical consciousness, so be it, a rose by any other name is still a rose.

The soul is the highest form of existence a human being can know. As far as one can tell, the universe of human souls is the apogee of the universe of being, including the entire inanimate universe, which latter is of no more interest than are the tellurian masses on earth. This is a cosmology relevant to conscious individuals, not the inhuman and irrelevant cosmology of astronomers. One can be infatuated for a time with the starry skies but it is only an infatuation; one of the forms of nature-love that humans are prone to adapt. This infatuation carried to extremes can become *inhumanism* (like that of the philosopher-poet Robinson Jeffers), a preference for unconscious nature and ultimately inanimate existence. This kind of attitude sooner or later leads to what the ancient labeled *misanthropy*, the contempt of humans, a condition amply demonstrated by Jeffers. A spiritual cosmology places individual humans at the center of the universe. One book by Søren Kierkegaard is worth more than a million astral photographs and the ensuing planetary maps. The life of Henry David Thoreau is far more significant than the revolutions of Jupiter. Perhaps humans need solar energy to survive but that does not mean undue emphasis be given to the sun; we also need to inspire oxygen to survive but we do not worship gaseous oxygen. It is our physical being that needs these things and if we do not know why our souls are wedded to the physical self, it is a reminder that we are not privy to all the secrets of the universe. What we do know is that our souls exist and this knowledge is infinitely more important than that of the bodies attached to them. Epictetus' definition of a human being was a soul dragging around a corpse. Those who pay more attention to the corpse than the soul are misguided persons who have been led astray by the seductive power of the senses. Such persons have always existed and will always exist but it is not necessary to take them too seriously.

The real self is the conscious soul. The important issues in human life are the spiritual issues derived from a cosmology that places souls in the center of the real universe instead of at the periphery of an artifactual one built out of superficial sense impressions. The materialist worldview misses the real universe of the spiritual individual; existence does precede essence but human existence is not just physiology, it is the soul's consciousness. No other form of reality is in the long run satisfying to the individual. In last analysis, philosophy is a matter of satisfying the soul.

A theocentric cosmology is no better for the individual than the Copernican one. It is the last refuge of those fearful of the consequences of their individuality. Theocentricity derives from human weakness that projects one's own responsibilities onto an almighty deity. The more one thinks he knows about God's will, the more one possesses sacred scriptures that explicate His will, the more He reveals himself through revelation—the more the universe centers on Him instead of us and we humans become his servants. The religious mystic goes further and seeks total union with Him. Christianity carried to its logical conclusion culminates in a Christocentric cosmology in which the souls of individuals are totally dependent on an image of a God they themselves have created. A bizarre situation! Even if the will of a powerful deity were to be somehow communicated to struggling individuals, it would not be a desirable event. The individual must realize himself, not the will of a Supreme Being existing in a different dimension of reality.

The great literature of the western world has always portrayed Lucifer—the arch individualist—in a more vivid and, truth to tell, more appealing manner than the heavenly hosts waiting upon the Lord. If Dante, Milton and Goethe had confined themselves to descriptions of the saved, it is most unlikely that any of them would have achieved the place they did in western literature. Their portrayal of devilish beings carry the authentic mark of individuality and, secretly or openly, are of greater interest to the reader than the wooden depictions of dutiful angels. We lose interest in Job as soon as he has made his peace with the Lord. It is individuality that marks the human spirit; the moment the individual bends his knee to an authority figure, divine or otherwise, his individuality diminishes and he is no longer the bearer of the vital spark that signifies the human condition.

It is hard to take seriously the specious claim that anyone has ever known anything about "God's will." Everything that has ever been said on this subject is certainly a human projection into a fantasized deity. This is evident in the religious attitude of primitives but somehow escapes civilized westerners in their own religions. All the traits and actions attributed to God, as Ludwig Feuerbach so methodically pointed out in *The Essence of Christianity*, are human traits and actions; when these derive from superior types of human beings, the notion of God is a superior type of God. The differences between Judaism, Christianity and Islam are the differences between Moses, Jesus and Mohammed. Worship of Jehovah, God or Allah is really worship of the individuals who claimed to reveal their will. Perhaps Christianity is the closest to reality because only it begins to make the identification of the prophet with deity.

The worship of anthropomorphic god-figures may serve to relieve the tension in the individual in dealing with his problems of existence but it is not in the best interests of his soul. All the spiritual development within society needs to be recapitulated in the individual; otherwise he is just a member of a flock instead of being an independent entity. The problem of worship phenomena in religions is that they tend toward the production of sheep, not humans. There are few features more striking in the history of Christianity than the tendency toward spiritual infantilism. Over and over again, the evangelist John appeals to his "little children" to be of good faith. The "children of God" are forever being ranged against the "children of Satan." In these juvenile contests, we are always told the good children will win out over the evil ones. If the metaphor is not of children, it is of servants; who will be the servant of God and who of the devil? But if one puts away material childish things, one does not want to take up spiritual childish things for when will one become a man? It is because of spiritual childishness that the true believers of Christianity assume the characteristics of perpetual mental childhood.

> Ja! Diesem Sinne bin Ich ganz ergeben,
> Das ist der Weisheit letzer Schluss:
> Nur der verdient sich Freiheit wie das Leben,

Der täglich sie erobern muss.
-- Goethe's *Faust*

Only he deserves freedom and life who daily conquers it by himself. Blind worshippers of doctrines no matter how inspired do not achieve life *kata syneidēsin;* somehow they have been led astray by Mephistopheles.

Perhaps it is arrogant to deny the existence of a higher power beyond human experience, but it is more arrogant to claim to a special connection with it. The ancient Hebrews felt it to be blasphemy to even pronounce the name of God; out of this feeling came the sacred tetragrammaton YHWH that was not to be pronounced by human voice. (Today television preachers can hardly say two sentences without recourse to the name of deity.) Of course, the Hebrews felt that their holy men had access to the mind of YHWH; moreover, they thought themselves to be His chosen people. But their instinct to avoid familiarity with divinity was well founded. Humans are far removed from the highest power, if they were not, they would not be human.

The altar to an unknown God in Athens described by the apostle Paul has already been mentioned. The account is important enough to merit reconsideration (Acts 17:16-32). The Athenians, at least some of them, familiar as they were with matters of philosophy and religion, must have felt the need to acknowledge a higher power in the universe. But they did not imagine that the human mind could penetrate all the spheres of existence. Even the quintessential materialist Epicurus envisioned Gods in the interstices of his atomic worlds, while denying any knowledge of their nature. The tribute to an Unknown God was the natural result of the Athenian religious sensibility acknowledging their awareness of a deity. They surely would have imagined their altar to have only a symbolic meaning; it is not evident why Paul should have accused them of worshipping the altar itself as if it were some kind of latter day golden calf. They might have pressed Paul to tell them how he knew more about God than they did but we will never know more than the brief scriptural account. We can imagine, however, that those who constructed the altar (*bōmon*, presumably a simple edifice) dispensed with the grandiose concepts of theocentric cosmologies—dogmatic righteousness, unlimited faith, infinite power—and merely acknowledged that there was more to heaven and earth than was conceived of in the philosophies and religions of antiquity.

It is really quite remarkable to think of the religious maturity that was required to dedicate an altar to an unknown god, dispensing with the dogmas that have usually possessed those with religious inclinations. It was a statement of religious humility, belying the opinion that the Greeks were prone to hubris. The hubris was all on the side of Paul whom the Athenians gently mocked, foregoing the more severe reactions that were his usual reward from other inhabitants of the Greco-Roman world—including his own fellow Jews. They even invited him to elaborate on his views! The religious tolerance attributed to the Athenians is astonishing considering the temper of the times; one can only guess what would have happened to a stranger appearing in a town after the establishment of Christianity who would have publically accused Christians of ignorance in their religious practices.

Acknowledgement of an unknown god does not lead to a theocentric cosmology. It necessarily leads to a cosmology centered on the soul since one cannot construct either an inner or an outer life on the dictates of an unknown god. The important word is 'unknown'; the god cannot be righteous, vengeful, loving or just; neither is he a father, a son, a light or a love, the god is simply apophatic, unknown. This limits the human tendency toward religious imaginativeness; one is no longer free to project his religiosity, thereby creating mental golden calves. He is forced to assume the burden of spiritual existence by himself and grapple with the tensions of fully conscious life. The only god it is legitimate for a conscious being to acknowledge is Agnōstō Theō, the unknown god. Thus agnosticism is not refusal to contemplate existence of a greater being, it is the recognition that the nature of this being cannot be known by him. Faith based solely on the desire for faith violates one's *intellectual conscience*, which must assert dominion over all emotional needs. The cosmology of a person with an agnostic attitude toward god centers on his own soul because to such a person, no other cosmology is possible.

When one is conscious of his own soul, he cannot help being conscious of the soul of others. His own consciousness derives originally from contact with the consciousness of others; culture is the means by which this self-other interaction occurs. But societies founded either upon a materialist or upon a theocentric worldview, with cosmologies in which inanimate being or suprahuman being are seen as the principal form of existence, and with styles of thought in which analytic reductionism or Gnostic imaginativeness take precedence over interior consciousness...no, such societies do not nurture growth of souls and need to be resisted with all the force available to the independent individual. The one thing needful has not changed and it is to the everlasting credit of the early Christian fathers that the importance of the soul was recognized and firmly established for over a thousand years in western culture. If we do not agree with Augustine that the only two questions for philosophy are those of the soul and of God, we are compelled to acknowledge that he was half right in his estimation (see Epilogue).

The individual who centers on his own soul cannot be a worshipper. His development originates from the experiences, reflections and expressions of his inner self. He is not narcissistically obsessed with his physical self, nor does he egotistically give himself over to the gratification of his will. Rather he is concerned with the development of his soul toward which he orients his interests and activities. His involvement with physical being, relationships and society fluctuates according to circumstances and his own temperament. However the one thing he desires above all else is the deepening of consciousness that signifies spiritual development. The purity of his heart depends on his willing of this one thing. His cosmology is *noocentric*, one centered on individual consciousness.

13. Intellectuals and Intellectuals Manqués

SELF-EXPRESSION TO NO purpose is the act of a deranged person. When we see some poor benighted soul lurching along a street, pontificating on a subject dear to his heart, without concern as to whether anyone is listening and not even appearing to be cognizant of his own thoughts, we feel a sudden pathos because this is a person with linguistic capacities, expending his energies to no evident purpose, accomplishing nothing for society or for himself. We expect nothing from him, we would not be surprised if he should relieve himself on the sidewalk or lie down amidst filth and excrement. Like a dog continually barking, he is a public nuisance and probably ultimately will be put away in a facility designed for such people.

The public expression of language requires a justifiable purpose. This not only includes oral expression but also written expression that, if not offensive to the ears, consumes endless paper and space, and in contemporary times, has become an avalanche of language overwhelming all facilities for the written word. The indiscriminate writer is a greater public menace than the street side rhetorician. Consequently the production of public language should be justified. As is well known, language serves various purposes for individuals. Without entering into all the ramifications of communication theory and psycholinguistics, it is possible to divide the use of language into two broad categories: communication and self-expression. Communication is directed toward an audience, one or many; self-expression arises from the interior self and does not require an audience. However, the difference between a mentally-ill individual pouring out a stream of meaningless language and a lonely writer transforming his intense feelings and ideas into written expression is often not easy to distinguish.

The key difference is *creating meaning*. The creative individual of every stripe gives meaning to the disorderly and contradictory chaos within himself, thereby forming his soul, while the madman only creates more chaos externally from his internal brand. Meaningful expressive writing that forms the soul in an admittedly mysterious manner goes a long way to explain the powerful drive to write seen in most creative writers. Self-expression has been long known to benefit the individual in various ways; physically, emotionally and psychologically. To this list may be added a fourth category; metaphysically, through giving form to his soul. There is no purpose in self-expression that is more important than this metaphysical one.

Language is the essential structural element of a deepened consciousness. One may define an individual for whom language serves preeminently as a means for forming his soul as an *intellectual*. One can go further and say that the intelligent (not intellectual) individual for whom language preeminently serves as a means of communication with society is an intellectual manqué, meaning that his intelligence has failed to fulfill its function *kata syneidēsin*. This does not disturb the intellectual manqué since in the contemporary world there is hardly any awareness of the soul.

Nothing appears more futile to the intellectual manqué than for his language to disappear into oblivion without obtaining societal recognition. He utilizes language in order to establish a position for himself at some societal level; the self-expressive purpose of the language is secondary to the utilitarian one. Self-expression is only as important as the number and importance of the people who take notice of it. Some intellectuals manqués may be principally concerned with the size of their audiences (a few thousand readers may be abject failure for an author accustomed to blockbuster successes), others judge their success by the importance of the attention their writings receive, e.g. prestigious reviews, analytical commentaries, literary prizes, etc. Ultimately, however, the common denominator of most intellectuals manqués is monetary remuneration.

The distinction between the intellectual and the intellectual manqué has been less clearly drawn in the past since the feeling used to be more prevalent that the use of the mind was a high calling that was its own reward and that, whatever its fate in the contemporary world, posterity could be relied upon to redress injustices. Posterity for intellectual writers was like heaven for Christians, the place where intelligence and literary ability would receive their due reward. In the present day, however, in the ruthlessly materialistic, unmetaphysically-minded western society, posterity and high callings have very little meaning. Communication is the characteristic most highly prized by the intellectual manqué who values his mental products strictly to the degree that they affect others. For him, this is the only purpose of literary work, this is what he thinks distinguishes his writings from the ineffectual activities of literary failures or the pointless outpourings of literary amateurs. Thus we have the high priest of the *non plus ultra* Frankfurt school of philosophy, Jürgen Habermas, concluding that the philosophy of mere consciousness has come to an end and what is now significant is the attainment of *Verständigung, intercomprehension.* Communication for Habermas is the true measure of validity of any idea and the achievement of consensus thinking is the final end of rational literary activity. Naturally, if there is no communication, there is no activity and the individual who does not enter into consensus is a non-being literarily speaking; a brute writing creature who has not entered into the established dialogues of society. This approach is much like that of the scientific world in which experiments that are not reported in reputable media can be regarded as having not been performed.

Doubtless, communication among like-minded individuals is a desirable feature in human affairs. But more important than communication is the soul of the communicator. Given a choice between greater thoughts without communication and lesser thoughts with communication, the individual who values his soul will always choose the former. The communication experts may pontificate that all feelings and ideas are communicable and it devolves upon the expressive individual to find the right means of communicating them. Experience teaches, however, that more often than not, the individual cannot find his audience without abandoning his individuality, selling his soul so to speak. Every intellectual, i.e. inner-directed person, sooner or later, reaches a crossroads at which he must decide whether his consciousness is to be pursued for its own sake or only to the extent that it can be apprehended and appreciated by others. There is no doubt about the attitude of the clerk-scholars of academia; no university faculty members can expect to survive if they do not compete successfully in the "publish or perish" environment characterizing the academic world.

It comes down finally to a matter of awareness and valuation of one's own soul. If one believes his soul is formed and strengthened through development of independent mental-spiritual faculties, then he will turn his efforts toward exercise of these faculties to the highest possible degree without concern for the reactions of the intellectual manqué guilds that exist everywhere. *It is more important to form a soul than to obtain a societal position.* Of course, if the very concept of a soul has no meaning for a person, the principle just expressed is meaningless. This person is an *intellectual manqué* because he has not achieved the level of development that results in consciousness of his own soul.

At the highest level, intellectuality and spirituality are identical attributes. Consciousness of one's interior being as a significant reality is the result of an intellectuality that has gone beyond executive skill cleverness. It is a matter of change in orientation. When Socrates tries to persuade Callicles in Plato's *Gorgias* that it is better to endure evil than to do evil because the latter would deform his soul, Socrates finally realizes that his efforts are hopeless. It was not that Callicles did not understand his argument or even (as Callicles admitted) that he was not attracted to the Socratic attitude, it was that the "love of *demos*"—society—dwelled in his soul and resisted Socrates. This love of *demos* dwells in the minds of all intellectuals manqués; were it not for that, orientation toward their own souls could not fail to emerge. The materialist worldview inevitably leads to the love of *demos* because there is no place in it for love of soul, and without that, the individual must turn to *demos* for his fulfillment.

Light years ago in the annals of American history, there occurred the phenomenon of the *pioneers*, bold individuals who had a vision of life based upon possession of land wrested from the wildernesses and prairies of America. The sagas of these individuals have been dramatized by writers like O.E. Rolvaag, Hamlin Garland and Willa Cather. One cannot indiscriminately idealize pioneer life; brave homesteaders exhibited the full panoply of human failings and vices. What is significant about them is that they lived by independent visions of their own. The ideal of self-reliance was paramount, enabling them to surmount incredible obstacles in search of a more fulfilling life. They worked their properties, raised their children and practiced their religions as best they could. When failures and catastrophes dogged their steps, as they often did, by and large they accepted their fate with resignation. It was not necessary for them to receive commendations, prizes, gifts, awards or other signs of societal approval. They had faith in their way of life in and of itself.

The intellectual is always a pioneer in some sense since he is carving out a way of life founded on his own soul. He is working his mind instead of his land. He may seem to be an impractical oddity to some (as did the pioneers) because he does not enter into the reward-no reward games that characterize society. Experiencing, learning, reflecting, expressing is enough for him because he has faith that his way of life is of value in itself and is necessary to form his soul. He will become aware that to the extent that he realizes his own soul, he will have withdrawn energies from society and therefore cannot expect societal reward for his behavior. Cliché though it may be, the timeworn saying that virtue is its own reward is nowhere more appropriate than in the formation of the soul.

There is, however, a common problem associated with the orientation toward personal development. Creative individuals run the risk of confusing the functions of society with those of the family. Families are social structures evolved by nature to give the young of a species a better chance of reaching adult life. They reward their young for developing behaviors conducive to survival. It is easy for creative types to see themselves in a similar relationship with society and are tempted to believe that society will take the place of the family that nature formed to ensure individual survival. They imagine that society will reward them for expressions founded on development of their consciousness.

Nothing could be further removed from reality. Society does not function as a family; it may feed starving people but does not reward individual spiritual development or expression. The individual who expects to sustain himself in a social system must participate in the social compact. Otherwise he is committing himself to a lottery in which the odds are heavily stacked against his winning. The likelihood that any intellectually oriented person, whatever his form of expression, will be supported by society is infinitesimally small. Societies are under no compulsion to reward individual spiritual merit, they only reward those who contribute to society according to societal values or interests prevalent at the time. Unfortunately, it is terribly difficult to develop the soul under conditions in which one's physical and psychological sustenance is uncertain. Intellectuality *kata syneidēsin* may be the highest function of the human condition, but its development is dependent upon the framework that supports it. Jean Améry in *Jenseits von Schuld und Sühne* has described how Auschwitz gave a crushing blow to metaphysics; confronted with club-wielding SS guards, the intellectual discovered the basis of existence was the availability of food, shelter and a humane environment.

Participation in the social compact means that one has something marketable to contribute to society. This is how the physical and psychological stability upon which higher development can occur is insured. Claude Bernard showed how stability of milieu is required for higher physiological functions; it is no less necessary for higher spiritual functions. The intellectual is not exempt from this requirement and it is no accident that most of the great individuals in culture developed themselves in situations that were secured by their own marketable skills. Without a special position in the world—which is less and less common in egalitarian societies—the individual can only assure his place in society through contributing to it. In this way, he frees himself for authentic spiritual and creative development without laboring under the burden of persuading anyone he should be supported in his more important task. There is nothing more detrimental to the soul's growth than for the individual to be seduced by the idea that society might support this process. The soul is a matter for the individual and it is he alone who must assure its welfare.

The ascetic lifestyles of the antique philosophers kept their material needs to a minimum, thereby permitting them considerable independence. Today's all but universal habituation to technology does not allow the way of life of a Socrates or Diogenes and the individual must devote more of his energies to mere survival. The person who fails to do this is the one most likely to eventually submit to the materialist outlook on life. Sooner or later, uncertainty causes only what is tangible to become real; food, house, clothing, automobile, money—especially money—anything that exists in object form, endowing it with a stabilizing influence. Desires and emotions become linked to the material world, which serves as the touchstone of reality. The soul does not share in this reality; the faith of the materialist lies in the tangibility of materia and whatever is outside of this frame of reference becomes merely insubstantial epiphenomena. It is not part of the "real" world.

The intellectual manqué feels that his societally-oriented concept of reality is the correct one because it best insures his material existence, inclusive of his intellectuality. Yet it is interesting that the previously cited Améry also reported that individuals committed to an ideal such as devout Jews or Christians, or even dedicated communists, endured Auschwitz much better than the skeptical intellectuals manqués (such as Améry himself). Those devoted to an ideal, no matter what its content, can endure deprivation better than materialists since they are not being deprived of what is most important to them. An ideal has no material qualities; anyone who has faith in an ideal to the degree that it will significantly affect his state of mind and behavior has an intimation of the human soul.

The unique ideal of Christendom is that God appeared on earth in human form. One might stretch this idea to envision that humans possess an element of divinity that reached a high point in the historical Jesus. To put it more concretely, a human being is a combination of the spiritual and material dimensions of being. This is an old scholastic preoccupation that needs refurbishing. No worldview that does not provide a proper perspective for both of these human attributes or gives mere lip service to one or the other is capable of advancing human welfare.

Archimedes is reputed to have claimed that if he were given an immovable platform, he could move the world. There is a tendency in humans to seek immovable platforms from which they can erect unshakable beliefs. For the materialist, the substantiality of the material object is the platform to movement of the world. Christianity asserted that there was more to existence than material being and emphasized the spiritual world within mankind. Unfortunately, Christians have tended to believe they too can move the material world through their faith. The most extreme form of this belief today is to be found in

Christian Science, which is the logical culmination of Christian faith. Supposedly if one aligns his soul with the absolute spiritual power of Christ, then "all things are possible." No Asian potentates or Spanish conquistadores ever reached quite the level of hubris of those who believe the mind of Christ can affect every aspect of existence. Cosmologies centered on founders rather than followers require miracles or other assertions of supernatural powers in order to be persuasive.

The preeminent function of the intellect is in the development of the individual's interior self. When the intellect is heedlessly given over to the service of skills, to the control of the material world or to the elaboration of Gnostic fantasies, it is a misuse of the highest human attribute. The Puritans in America understood the dangers of a materialism run amok and tried to take measures to insure its appropriate place in their society. We may differ with the Puritans in assigning control of the intellect to the individual rather than to authoritarian social laws. We may question bible worship and reliance on supposed knowledge of God's will. However we must wonder if they were on the right track toward a higher realization of the human condition, especially when we compare their mentality with that of present day society. So too on the right track was Père Teilhard de Chardin when he wrote in *Le Milieu Divin:*

> In its highest degree of generality, the doctrine of the Cross is that to which every man adheres who comes to believe that the immense agitations of human life

open onto a road that has a goal and that this road *ascends.* Life has a conclusion: therefore, it imposes a direction toward which it orients itself; specifically, toward the highest possible spiritualization through the greatest possible effort.

"The highest possible spiritualization"—no better formulation can be found for the human effort. The road is so difficult, however, that no unnecessary materialist or metaphysical baggage can be carried along.

14. Philosophical Faith

"FAITH IS NOTHING ELSE than belief in the absolute reality of subjectivity." So stated Ludwig Feuerbach in his nineteenth century book *The Essence of Christianity* whose epochal concepts have yet to be incorporated into western culture. The title is somewhat misleading; the title Feuerbach originally proposed was "Critique of Pure Irrationality, the Correspondence of Religion with the Essence of Mankind," a ponderous title but one that is descriptive of its contents. Marketing problems, however, led Feuerbach's publisher to utilize the title under which it appeared, apparently with Feuerbach's consent. The book is now generally to be found in the religious section of bookstores.

It is noteworthy that about the time Feuerbach's book appeared, two other writers were producing their own epochal books with very different styles and interpretations but essentially endorsing the theme that subjectivity is what counts. These were Henry David Thoreau

(*Walden*) and Søren Kierkegaard (*Concluding Unscientific Postscript*) whose lives and works were based on this belief. None of these writers knew of the existence of the others yet certain ideas in their work were astonishingly similar. Something in the *Zeitgeist* of the mid-nineteenth century was generating the intuition that "truth is subjectivity."

In the contemporary era, there is little evidence that such an intuition has survived. The world is still bedeviled with the age-old habits of projecting the feelings of the inner self into outer objects of worship, if not a demanding Jehovah, than a stylish home or a state of the art automobile. Islam is on the rise, threatening to displace the traditional Christianity of western societies. Individuals are still not capable of justifying their spirituality within themselves; there needs to be an external power or tradition legitimizing its existence. European philosophy as a guide to a higher life has been a failure and is now confined to university existence with identification of philosophers as historians, teachers or cognitive 'scientists'—in spite of the tirades of Schopenhauer and Nietzsche. Those philosophy professors who wish to express themselves on the human condition are now more inclined to demonstrate against racism or attack 'savage' capitalism than to speak to the issue of interior consciousness.

The individual who wishes to develop his soul, however, needs something more than political activism. He needs a way of life that is founded on his own subjectivity. The ancient Greeks did not feel it necessary to add that the *gnōthi seauton* would not occur without the *experiences* that teach the individual about himself. No one develops a fruitful subjectivity locked in a closet; the Puritans carrying the mission of the Reformation into a hostile wilderness had plenty of experiences through which their souls could grow. By the time of Emerson and Thoreau, however, it was becoming evident that American civilization could interfere with the experiences and reflections necessary for inner growth.

One might maintain that the art of human life lies in fostering the types of experiences that lead to interior development. Only the individual himself can intuit what kind of experience will be meaningful to him; what will lead to deepening of the soul in one individual may be tedious drudgery for another. Fulfillment for Thoreau came from solitary roaming in the woods of Concord; for Feuerbach, it was an intimate relationship with a young woman of exceptional spiritual qualities. Kierkegaard's formative experience in life was being son to a remarkable father; however one views this relationship, it left its imprint on Kierkegaard's soul. One might add the self-evident fact that fulfilling human experiences must involve one's physical being since the human condition does not permit any other means of experiencing the world.

Faith is more than a cognitive act of 'believing,' it is a commitment of the self to an attitude toward existence. Faith in the material world or faith in an exterior God or faith in one's own soul all create different attitudes toward existence that affect every fiber of one's being. Humans cannot really live without any faith at all, although they can live without a metaphysical belief system. The gravest predicament in life, one that can lead to self-destruction, is to be left stranded without a faith. Faith is integral, it cannot be split into parts; the development of belief in one god instead of many gods was universally recognized as a higher type of religious belief. There is no logical reason why there should be only one god; there are many planetary bodies, why not many gods? But something in the human psyche led to monotheism as minds matured. Perhaps this is because the source of religious sensibility is the integral human soul.

Dedication to one's own soul is as religiously significant as any faith in god. It is awareness of the sacredness of spirituality that is the essential attribute of religion; the particular configuration of this spirituality is of less import. The configuration of spirituality must conform to only one law, the law of reality that requires that any type of consciousness, of which spirituality is one, conform to real instead of imaginary existence. *Homo sapiens* possess an *intellectual conscience* to enforce the law of reality. Belief in an almighty power with definable attributes and desires does not conform to that law. I do not know whether or in what form God exists but I do know that I exist and possess an interior spiritual reality called the soul. My faith is dedicated to this reality. There is no need for a spiritual metaphysics located outside of myself (see Epilogue). Nor can I exactly define the nature of this interior self that variably manifests itself as emotionality, desire, will or most importantly, intelligent consciousness.

Consciousness is not a static state but changes kaleidoscopically in its content and orientation. It may be affected by a moral sense in which case it is called conscience. It is not important to produce a Gray's Anatomy of consciousness as the savants of phenomenology have tried to do. Consciousness in all its dimensions ought not be an object of scholarly investigation; it is something to aspire toward with all one's energies. If purity of heart is to will one thing as Kierkegaard said, then the will toward consciousness is the philosopher's claim to internal purity.

When one contemplates the course of human history, the prospects do not appear bright for *Homo sapiens kata syneidēsin.* People seem more inclined to develop themselves as conquerors of nature than as devotees of their souls. It is hard to avoid the feeling that spiritual consciousness is disappearing. Christianity, the major religious force in the world to date, has not provided a consciousness of spirituality that conforms to the requirement of reality. Christian faith, Christian hope and Christian love are spiritual states but they are anchored to a cosmology that is no longer believable. God is dead as a real force in the world for too many individuals. However, the materialist worldview, which is devoid of spirituality, is eminently believable. Nature is a tangible reality affecting the human state in many ways and science has learned how to successfully deal with nature. The more scientific technologies enter into the daily framework of human life, the more individuals become fixed to a materialist worldview. For those with a spiritual bent of mind, the human condition is unpromising. Robinson Jeffers felt that the human race was a failed experiment of nature; he concluded that a new start with a new model was needed.

But the single individual *qua* individual has nothing to do with the human race or any other abstraction referring to multitudes whether the numbers are in the dozens or the billions. Even the family is an abstract concept without in-depth reality as far as the single individual is concerned. The unprecedented murderous violence of the German Third Reich could not be assimilated by individuals when presented as so many millions of people tortured, gassed or shot. Viewing pictures was more significant and visiting concentration camps even more so. But most significant of all was the experience of incarceration in the camps, which was an experience that changed the consciousness of the survivors forever.

The proper study of mankind is man, the proper study of the individual is the self. Man the historian studies the course of mankind, man the individual studies himself—or other selves that teach him about himself. *Gnōthi seauton* (know yourself) is still the first and most important commandment of spiritual existence. The shifting currents of humanity on this planet are like the galaxies in the universe, they may be of interest from an abstract point of view but of no real significance for the individual. All the races, religions and nations of man have no more meaning to me than do the extinct dinosaurs or the unborn races yet to emerge. This attitude called 'nominalism' by medieval scholastics is founded on the preeminence of individual existence, which is the main criterion by which individuals should regulate their lives.

The scriptural injunctions that Jesus identified as most important for right living were first to love God with all one's strength and second to love one's neighbor as one's self. But Jesus went beyond the scriptures; he asserted that the kingdom of heaven was *within* the individual. We must assume that Jesus did not regard his assertion as morally defective egocentricity; we think that he was announcing a new dimension in human spiritual history. Human activities based on external affairs are not part of this dimension; they are part of the world of externality that dominates other life forms. To be born again is to become spiritual, to turn inward. Society, family, occupation—all these have to do with the exterior self no matter how important they may seem. But when one turns within, a new world is found without limits; it is only necessary to have the willingness and the determination to explore it.

Philosophical faith is faith in the soul as the most important aspect of human existence. Subjectivity is not merely the antithesis of objectivity; it is consciousness of the internal dimension that is the special terrain of humanness. It is impossible to look within and without simultaneously with the same degree of intensity. When totally concentrating on the

object world, the interior dimension contracts and ultimately disappears. The person whose energies are habitually turned toward objectivity does not feel this dimension and regards it as illusory. If one's gaze is continually fixed on the outer world, he is confined to that world. The interior "kingdom" is perceptible only to those with the will and ability to fix a steady gaze upon it.

This discussion may seem to resemble a religious tract more than a philosophical statement. But there is no claim for a higher sanction for these thoughts; they entirely represent a personal intuition of the nature of human existence. No god or holy spirit or evil power (hopefully not) is at work. The writing is the outcome of the expressive energies of the writer that wish to see the light of day. The fact that they have some kinship with Christian consciousness is evidence that there is a common reality, a shared *Logos*, which all spiritually oriented individuals carry. However, the writer feels no obligation to carry the excess baggage of Christianity, whether it be a brief Apostle's Creed or all the pronouncements of the Roman Catholic Church, *ex cathedra* and *urbi et orbi*, during two millennia of Christian history. Nor is he inclined to accept the bibliolatry of the Protestant sects since, to him, the thoughts of Jesus are a philosophical treasure from a human being like himself to be used according to his own lights. He is no more disposed to worship them than to worship any other treasure.

The essential element of philosophical faith is to trust the intuitions of the interior self; this makes it the most difficult of all faiths. However, a faith that is dependent upon societal traditions is not real faith. Faith has been defined by a noted antique writer as "the conviction of things not seen"; as such, the presence of religious symbols, music or monuments, the emotional rewards of religious fellowship and, most especially, the derivation of concrete benefits from religious protestation do not strengthen faith, they corrupt it. One cannot speak of faith in an enterprise from which one obtains visible benefits. We live in an absurd world in which individuals say they have faith in activities that richly reward them. Levels of existence cannot be mixed any more than metaphors; it is improper to talk of faith when faith is providing material or social rewards to the individual.

The pioneer Puritans deceived themselves when they thought communal faith could be supported by visibly exposing the faithless in wooden stocks. Faith that cannot be maintained except through tangible rewards or punishments is not faith; it is adaptation to the environment. One must adapt to his environment but there is no point in calling such adaptation by other names. Kierkegaard recognized the absence of genuine faith in contemporary Christendom; it is difficult to understand why he persisted in trying to resuscitate a faith that was—and is—dependent on dogmas that are as defunct as any of the antique philosophical schools of Athens. When there is no viable basis to faith, faith *kata syneidēsin* becomes defunct itself.

Philosophical faith is a consciousness of and trust in one's own soul. Consciousness of soul inevitably leads to concern for its wellbeing. There is very little in contemporary society to support wellbeing of the soul; one must create it, Don Quixote-like, driven by a personal intuition rather than by conformity. Miguel de Unamuno said of Don Quixote that he taught the world how the individual spirit rises above ridicule and rejection. The image of the undaunted knight is one toward which an individual with soul can aspire; it is only through renunciation of approval by society and distaste for its rewards that he is enabled to come to philosophical faith and thereby form his own soul.

FINIS

Epilogue - 2nd Edition

SINCE THE FIRST EDITION of *Souls Exist (1989)* is now out of print and the issues with which it deals are as relevant as ever, it seems appropriate to make a new edition available. My conviction that souls exist as metaphysical realities is unchanged. But I would like to provide a supplement to the new edition. The epigraph of the first edition quotes St. Augustine: "There are only two questions for philosophy; the soul and God." In my introduction at that time, I narrowed this list down to one, the soul. I thought God was a subject not pertinent to philosophy. I would like to withdraw that reservation because now I agree with Augustine that the concept of God is a subject pertinent to philosophy, albeit I have little else in common with his approach to theological matters. In actual fact, the first edition of this book contains considerable discussion of the significance of negative or apophatic theology.

My change in attitude is in no way related to any revelation from a supreme deity, since I have never had nor ever expect to have any such revelation. It is entirely based upon my effort at lucidity in consideration of the assertion that souls exist. I believe that the existence of an individual metaphysical soul with no metaphysical connections of any sort to the universe is an absurdity. I have become convinced that the soul as an existent metaphysical reality requires a metaphysical substratum. The German mystic Jacob Boehme called this substratum *Der Ungrund*, the groundless, the fecund source of everything that exists. Alternatively, in my opinion, it may be called 'God.'

The idea that physiological processes can be transformed into a soul requires a miracle analogous to transforming bread and wine into the body and blood of Christ. One's intellectual conscience should forbid believing in such miracles. There is no $E = mc^2$ for transforming metabolism of the brain into spiritual existence. Without a metaphysical substratum, the soul is unimaginable to me. This concept has long been an established tenet of Christianity. (Acts 17:28) It should not be forgotten that Paul was speaking in Greek to a Greek audience of philosophers and quoting from the Greek philosopher-poet Epimenides to make his point. The particular formulation or language one prefers is a matter of tradition, education and temperament. In scholastic terminology, these thoughts come under the category of 'natural theology' (reason, experience) as contrasted with 'revealed theology' (revelation, Scripture). I limit myself to the former category.

One may wonder if an anlage for every human soul exists in this metaphysical substratum, requiring a human individual to become fully formed. One can even speculate that without such formation, 'God' cannot be fulfilled. However, there should be a limit to metaphysical speculation. The exact nature of the relationships between the soul, the human body and the universe will forever remain a mystery to the human mind. It is just as well that the metaphysical excesses of scholastic philosophy reached their appointed end long ago.

Thoughtful scientists no longer hold the idea that the mind is an illusory epiphenomenon arising from biochemical or electrical processes in the brain. Modern physics has revealed unknown dimensions of existence; dogmatic monism has become intellectually and philosophically outdated. But the dimension known as the soul could hardly exist as an aberrant isolate unrelated to the surrounding cosmos. Just as the human body could not exist unrelated to the laws of physics, chemistry and biology, so the human soul must require a connection to the metaphysical dimensions of existence. One's intellectual conscience should forbid *not* believing in some form of this connection.

There is a remarkable verse by the seventeenth century Catholic convert Angelus Silesius that bears quoting in the original German (*Der Cherubinische Wandersmann*):

> *Ich weiss, dass ohne mich Gott nicht ein*
> *Nu kann leben—*

Werd ich zu nicht, er muss von Not den Geist aufgeben.

I know that God cannot live one instant without me,
If I should come to naught, He must cease to be.

Er lebt in mir, He lives in me. I do not have sufficient self-confidence to endorse this belief but I don't reject it either. How Angelus Silesius escaped the stake, I do not know.

The Russian existentialist philosopher Nikolai Berdyaev authored one of the most profound works of the contemporary era loosely entitled in English *Solitude and Society*. The exact translation of the Russian title would be "I and the World of Objects." A better English title would have been "I, Spirituality and the World of Objects." A similar triangulation; *Ichsein, Dusein and Essein*—Ego, Thou and It—was described by Martin Buber in his classic book, *I and Thou*. The working out of these issues is at the core of the problem of human existence. Personal philosophy, not dogmatic theology, is needed for this process since individuals must grasp the meaning of such ideas for themselves. They do not need a savior in human form who only blurs the issues. Nor do they need an overpowering array of rituals, traditions and authority figures, which also blur them.

I have reached a point in my intellectual development in which my conscience requires me to believe in the reality of an ultimate substratum of spiritual existence. Perhaps a more original term than 'God' could be found for this substratum, free from all the misuses of the past. No one has spoken to me from above; I have had to converse with myself. Philosophy is the high conversation of the soul. I find these thoughts to be liberating and preferable to imagining 'grace' has arrived from elsewhere.

Belief in an ultimate reality seems to naturally take root in my soul, once the bar of intellectual conscience is lifted. There is a unique satisfaction arising from this thought. No legends, intermediaries or imaginary constructs about God's will are necessary; it is enough for me to believe there is an ultimate reality connected to my existence. I don't feel that the term *love* is appropriate for my relationship with this reality. *Reverence* seems to be the emotion that is called for; reverence for it as well as reverence for my soul.

Those who might read this entire book may feel that I have fallen victim to a psychological malady well known to antiquity—that of the hubris mentioned above. I will admit that this thought has occurred to me on more than one occasion. But this writing was composed years ago in response to an inner compulsion to expression that I could not deny and which I will not deny now. Let the *Moirai* decide its fate.

I will end this discussion by putting forth five thoughts I think worthy of expression:

1) The interior self becomes spiritualized in the course of life. This occurs by means of experiences, reflection and vitality. A metaphysical substratum of spiritual existence, whether acknowledged or not, is an essential factor for this process to come to fruition.

2) Creativity in all its forms is the purest expression of the soul, taking precedence over all other virtues. Creativity is the one aspect of human life that is entirely spiritual.

3) When concern with the material world entirely displaces spirituality, human beings contract into material beings. Human life is not fulfilled.

4) If the pernicious illusion that one knows the will of God enters into the mind, religious fanaticism takes hold of the individual and perverts the soul.

5) The human soul strives to become conscious of its place in the vast surround of eternity outside of space and time— speaking religiously, of its place in God— and thus can relinquish the desire for temporal immortality.

These statements could be elaborated upon, but would lead me beyond the proper limits of an epilogue.

The framework of the first edition of *Souls Exist* has not been altered, except for some corrections and additions. The writing was a product of a state of mind at an earlier time in my life and any major changes would probably damage it. Furthermore, there was a mood to the first writing that cannot be regained. August Strindberg once wrote that he hardly ever altered his writings for fear of ruining them. It is an attitude with which I sympathize.

A reader of this new edition is referred to the last paragraph of the original introduction, which still accurately represents my feelings about *Souls Exist*.

I now wish to express my appreciation to the late Dick Ellington whose expert typesetting and wise advice made the original version of this work possible. At least equally important has been the tireless support of my wife Melanie Dreisbach whose many contributions to this book were essential to its creation.

Paris, 2012